# TOWARDS AN AESTHETIC OF OPPOSITION

## ESSAYS ON LITERATURE CRITICISM & CULTURAL IMPERIALISM

### ARUN MUKHERJEE

## Williams-Wallace Publishers
Ontario Canada

Published in
Williams-Wallace Publishers Inc.
P.O. Box 756
Stratford, Ontario, Canada
N5A 4A0
Copyright © 1988 Arun Prabha Mukherjee

ISBN: 0-88795-068-X     W

Canadian Cataloguing in Publication Data

Mukherjee, Arun Prabha, 1946-
Towards an Aesthetic of Opposition

ISBN 0-88795-068-X

1. Canadian literature - South Asian - Canadian authors - History and criticism. 2. Canadian literature - South Asian authors - History and criticism. I. Title.

PS8089.5.S68M84   1988   C810'.9'8914   C88-093236-8
PR9188.2.S68M84   1988

Published with the generous assistance of the Canada Council and the Ontario Arts Council

Printed and bound in Canada

Typesetting: Sarah Rashid Communication Services
Cover: Patrick White
Printing by Hignell Printing

# CONTENTS

1.  Introduction............................................4

2.  The Vocabulary of the "Universal":
    The Cultural Imperialism of the Universalist
    Criteria of Western Literary Criticism......................10

3.  Ideology in the Classroom:
    A Case Study in the Teaching of English
    Literature in Canadian Universities ........................23

4.  The Poetry of Michael Ondaatje and Cyril Dabydeen:
    Two Responses to Otherness ............................32

5.  South Asian Poetry in Canada:
    In Search of a Place .....................................52

6.  The Sri Lankan Poets in Canada:
    An Alternative View ......................................69

7.  *Digging Up the Mountains:*
    Bissoondath's Doomed World............................84

8.  The Poetry of Rienzi Crusz:
    Songs of an Immigrant..................................90

9.  The Third World in the Dominant Western
    Cinema: Responses of a Third World Viewer ...............100

# Introduction

These essays are written by a person who was born and brought up in post-colonial India, had a thoroughly colonial education, both in India and at the University of Toronto in Canada, and then went through a painful and difficult process of decolonisation. The essays record the dialectics of that struggle. In a sense, it is a collective struggle, being waged in the hearts and minds of all Third World people.

My education, like that of most of my generation, had been from top down. Knowledge trickled down to us from the west and we paid respectful homage to every printed word that bore a western name. When we did not understand something — and there was a lot that did not make sense — we blamed ourselves for our lack of knowledge.

Thus, a canon made mostly of ahistorical and apolitical Anglo-American texts was presented to me as the epitome of what constituted literature. It did not educate me in anything and alienated me from my reality. It made me believe that literature pertained to the cultivation of certain emotions — sentimental effusions over the beauty of nature, anguish over mutability — and a high-minded disdain for all rationality and abstract thought.

My Canadian education did not remove any cobwebs. Professors and fellow-students seemed to talk *ad infinitum* about symbolism and imagery, trace elaborate structures and patterns that persistently remained invisible to me. Every hero and heroine seemed to go on a quest of discovery of self-identity in their discourses. The other thing these heroes did was to go through initiation of some sort. At times it was called rites of passage. And yes, there were some other themes: modern sensibility, i.e., the pain of living in a Godless universe, wilderness versus civilization and their endless pulls, creativity versus madness, and, finally, the celebration of complexity that perpetually wrings its hands in the face of the grandeur and terror of the universe. Their reiteration soon made me realize that the reason the trickle of knowledge that I had drunk from in India had not made sense to me was not because there was more of it that I did not know but because the trickle remained substantively the same even when I stood close to the fount.

To discover intricate patterns for their own sake has never interested me. However, one churned out the kind of papers that one was asked for if one wanted to get through a highly punitive and exclusive system.

In order for these petty, irresponsible and elitist schemes to work, the curriculum is so chosen as to exclude or ghettoise dissonant discourses. In India, the United States Information Service provided us, free of charge, American literature anthologies edited by Robert E. Spiller et al. F O. Matthiessen's *The American Renaissance* was the other text that the U.S.I.S. supplies in multiple copies to our departmental library.

As a result, I imbibed an attitude that American writers were all latter day Romantics, communing with nature and leading a conflict-free life in a beautiful land. Without any historical background, I read *The Adventures of Huckleberry Finn* and took it to be another idyll. The historical traumas of slavery and the fate of the native peoples were kept obscure from my mind.

University of Toronto did not shake me out of my misconceptions. Here, too, one studied about poets and novelists who wrote about the travails of the spirit, their yearning for a lost paradise, their disgust with modern times etcetera. We were constantly told to remember that "it isn't what you say but how you say it that's important." What you say is not important, apparently, because themes are supposedly perennial — love, hate, coming of age, cycles of nature, death.

Obviously, the themes of history — conquest and subjugation, anti-colonial struggles, racism, sexism, class conflict — are all absent from this world view. Hence, the works that deal with this world view are also largely absent from the curricula of departments of English in Canada. The shrines at which they worship are to be seen in their course offerings. T.S. Eliot, Henry James, James Joyce, Ezra Pound, Robert Frost, Wallace Stevens dominate modern literature curricula.

Hegemony is thus achieved, on the one hand by a careful selection of artists and, on the other hand, it is achieved by neglecting the socio-political contexts and concentrating exclusively on technique. Elsewhere, I have examined in greater detail the distortions this kind of attention to technique, completely isolated from context, creates. [1] The text is read passively, on its own terms and never for identifying the exclusions or affiliations it exercises.

When these halls of learning do open up to such fields as Commonwealth literature, Black literature, Women's Studies, they do two things to them. On the one hand, these courses are marginalized in various ways so that the students know in no uncertain terms their relative unimportance in the scheme of things, and, on the other, their effectiveness is undermined because they are often taught and written about using the same ahistorical methods I have mentioned earlier. A majority of the white critics writing and teaching about Third World writers flatten them down to their image patterns, mythic archetypes, allusions, intertextuality, east-west conflict and, ultimately, universality.

I want to say here, as so many other voices of the Third World are saying, this condescending and ignorant approach is tiresome. We are tired of being told what is great literature and how it ought to be read. We are amazed how these institutions of learning in the west go on ignoring our responses to western literature and literary criticism. We are astonished at the way they choose to read and distort the cultural productions of the Third World artists.

In *Harder They Come,* Michael Thelwell describes how the young audience in the slums of Jamaica appropriate the Hollywood Western to suit their own needs. "The movies were still a great part of their scene, but now they shouted for the Indians and never took the white man's side, much less his name."[2] A similar rereading and appropriation or rejection of western canonical texts is a very important aspect of the oppositional critical activity going on in the Third World.

Another aspect of Third World literary and critical activity is the creation of new artistic modes that break away from the western artist-as-hero-creating-in-the-isolation-of-his-soul type of works. The Third World artists create to give voice to the experience of their community, to bring to life the historic memory and to explore the future. They deliberately reject the ahistorical western modes. Thus, in *Meridian,* a novel of struggle and pride of identity, Alice Walker's comment subtly brings out the difference between the two modes of creativity: "Anne-Marion, she knew, had become a well-known poet whose poems were about her two children, and the quality of the light that fell across a lake she owned."[3]

These oppositional critiques are winning audiences, whether the gatekeepers of the universitites admit them or not. There are only two ways to go. One is to listen and debate; perhaps both sides will change and learn in that process. The other, the one that prevails now, is to pretend that no other voices speak and to continue to teach, read, and write in one's hermetically sealed box. Let the Black parents scream about racism in *The Adventures of Huckleberry Finn.* We will continue to teach it as a classic. And we will continue to exclude texts that the Blacks themselves have written. And, yes, we will talk about the spectre of censorship when we hear such talk.

The essays collected in this volume have all emerged in a combative spirit. The stance of establishment literary criticism in North America is appreciative. The literary critics choose the works that have engaged them and then carry on detailed analyses, never doubting for a moment that what pleases them may not please everybody else. Thus, an upper middle class, usually male and white, point of view is presented with the authority of the universal. I, of course, do not have that authority. I cannot afford to speak in a calm and collected voice. The stance of these essays is confrontational not out of choice but out of necessity. I have tried to point out how the dominant discourse in North America dehistoricizes and depoliticizes everything so that non-white, non-male, working class ways of apprehending reality seldom get a hearing.

Though the essays speak for themselves, it would be helpful if the reader knew the context they emerged from. While the arrangement in the book is tactical, here I would like to pursue the chronological link.

"Two Responses to Otherness: The Poetry of Michael Ondaatje and Cyril Dabydeen" came out of a project on South Asian writing in Canada. The paper emerged only because I was forced to place Ondaatje in the context of other South Asian writers active in Canada. I began to ask questions like why no other South Asian writer had received the critical attention bestowed on Ondaatje by Canadian white critics? Why had they not bothered to check reviews by fellow Sri Lankans? Why no other South Asian writers had well-known publishers and fancy get-up? The paper is an attempt to seek out for myself the factors that would attract white critics to Ondaatje's work.

"South Asian Poetry in Canada: In Search of a Place" and "Songs of an Immigrant: The Poetry of Rienzi Crusz" were completed after "Two Responses to Otherness," although the research and mental processes evident in the three essays belong to the same spectrum. The three papers, I believe, are complementary, and some of the unstated meanings and assumptions will become clear to the reader simply through juxtaposing the three.

"The Sri Lankan Poets in Canada: An Alternative View" emerged from similar concerns and was written on the invitation of the guest editor of *The Toronto South Asian Review's* special issue on Sri Lanka. Once again, placing Ondaatje in a group setting brought out questions that would remain muted if one focussed on the single author. Here I also wanted to examine the damaging impact of western critical assumptions on the creativity of Third World writers.

"The Vocabulary of the 'Universal': Cultural Imperialism in Western Literary Criticism" was written in the white heat of anger that I felt upon reading the quotation from Northrop Frye that was chosen as the theme for the 1984 conference of Canadian Association for Commonwealth Literature and Language Studies (CACLALS). I felt that the whole conference was being based on the assumption that Third World literary works could be read as derivative and inter-textually linked with the works of the western European tradition.

"Ideology in the Classroom: A Case Study in the Teaching of English Literature in Canadian Universities" was written right after the article on cultural imperialism. I was frustrated by the essays my students at the University of Regina had turned out on a very political story by Margaret Laurence and the paper was an attempt at clarification for myself and, I hoped, for others. For if one cannot communicate one's point of view to others, one hasn't really clarified anything.

"*Digging Up the Mountains:* Bissoondath's Doomed World" was done as a book review for *World Literature Written in English.* The conventions of a book review determined the form of the writing and I did not bring in some of the issues bothering me about Neil Bissoondath. Once again, I find it interesting that after Ondaatje, only Bissoondath has managed to find a reputable Canadian publisher. Once again, the Canadian literary community has showered a lot of attention. Bissoondath was also considered good enough to be chosen as a finalist for a prestigious award. I find it curious that the fact of his being V.S. Naipaul's nephew was loudly announced on the dust jacket of the book as well as taken up in the reviews. I would have liked the discussion to be based on the questions dealing with his art and the politics he projects through his work.

I believe that the context of any writing is important. When I presented these papers at conferences, many unspoken issues came out in the discussions afterwards. I wonder why those issues should emerge only informally and not be written about so that a frank and open discussion can take place across the board. The information I have provided in this Introduction escaped the reach of the written word because of the conventions one must follow if one wants to be listened. Ultimately, one's audience decides how one will write.

I am thankful to journals like *JCL, WLWE* and *TSAR* for providing space for an alternative point of view. I am also thankful to organizations like CACLALS that are open to marginalized people and marginalized issues in ways larger professional organizations of university academics in my discipline are not. The essays collected here would not have seen the light of day but for these forums.

Finally, I am thankful to Ann Wallace, who considers these essays important enough to be collected and published in book form. Her publishing house, Williams-Wallace, is the right place for the collection to come out from: along with works by other people of colour, discovering their history, rediscovering their identity, and struggling for their just place in Canadian society. This book is a part of that collective struggle.

## NOTES

[1] Arun Mukherjee, *The Gospel of Wealth in the Modern American Novel: A Study of Dreiser and Some of His Contemporaries.* (London, Sydney: Croom Helm, 1987).

[2] Michael Thelwell, *Harder They Come.* (New York: Grove Press, 1980).

[3] Alice Walker, *Meridian.* (New York: Pocket Books, 1976).

*To*
*Alok*
*Friend and Husband*

# The Vocabulary of the "Universal":
## The Cultural Imperialism of the Universalist Criteria of Western Literary Criticism

*I feel that there is something being hidden by the terms "indigenous" and "metropolitan," or rather there is some thing not being said. In my view, the real terms are "national democratic" cultures and "imperialist" cultures, and the real tension is between the national cultures of Africa — or the national cultures of Third World peoples — and the imperialist cultures of Japan, Western Europe and the United States.*

*Ngugi Wa Thiong'o*

Though Commonwealth literature can claim to have given rise to a tremendous critical activity on the part of western critics during the last decade and a half, one would not be simplifying too much if one were to say that much of this criticism boils down to a rather repetitive discussion of two issues: the debt the works of the new Commonwealth owe to the western literary tradition and their "universality." Indeed, the two issues seem to have divided the Commonwealth family into two opposing camps which could be defined as western European versus Afro-Asian, the latter group maintaining that the western critics, instead of developing a sensitivity to other ways of apprehending the world, have simply imposed the traditional western categories on the works from the new Commonwealth, all in the name of "universality." In his "Thoughts on the African Novel," Achebe describes this mentality as "the dogma of universality." Taking issue with Eldred Jones' evaluation of Soyinka whom Jones considers to be portraying "a universal problem" in *The Interpreters,* Achebe writes:

> For supposing 'events all over the world' have *not* shown 'in the new generation a similar dissatisfaction...' would it truly be invalid for a Nigerian writer seeing a dissatisfaction in *his* society to write about it? Am I being told, for Christ's sake, that before I write about any problem I must first verify whether they have it too in New York and London and Paris?[1]

Achebe is denying validity to those interpretations which praise or criticise works on the basis of universality.[2] Achebe is also denying the liberal humanist

10

position that things in Nigeria must be the same as they are in New York, London and Paris since all human beings belong to the one big family called humanity. And finally, Achebe is denying another sacred liberal humanist assumption which believes that good literature concerns itself with universals by claiming that he is going to address himself to the differences between Nigerians and the people residing in New York, London and Paris.

Achebe's views on these issues are by no means exceptional. Several Afro-Asian writers have voiced objections against what has been considered western cultural imperialism. Nevertheless, the universalist criteria continue to be used in western literary criticism, and the users seem to imply high praise when they deem a Commonwealth writer to have universal appeal.

Though "universal" is a valorized term in the western liberal humanist criticism, its use in the Afro-Asian context leads to certain misrepresentations and evasions. As Achebe's comments indicate, universalist criteria totally overlook the historical, time and place specific experience of a people in their insistence that life in Nigeria is more or less similar to life in the metropolitan centres of the western world because of the essential brotherhood of man. The local and the specific are mere layers to the universalist critic underneath which can be discerned the archetypes of human drama. The following passage from an article published in *World Literature Written in English* is a good example of this type of criticism:

> [P]olitics is not the motivating force or central concern of his work. Naipaul recreates the political conflicts and tensions to be true to the ethos of the society he writes about and to create . . . a dramatic backdrop that serves to heighten his protagonists' personal conflicts and tensions. He does not make politics his exclusive thematic concern nor does he restrict himself to national issues. Naipaul's is a cosmopolitan, internationalist consciousness, which surveys com passionately the human condition, not restrictively the political, the racial or the national. [2]

Ramraj devalues the political, racial and national while valorizing the cosmopolitan and the international. Once he has established his hierarchies, he sets out to criticise writers (Achebe is named specifically) who write about local politics as "publicists," and accuses them of "moral flabbiness."[3]

Thus, the universalist criteria are subtly selective: they prefer the writers who downplay the local and the specific as opposed to the writers engaged in portraying the day to day life of their societies as participants. Helen Tiffin comments that "an orthodoxy has developed which dismisses realist writers as inherently inferior to those with more overtly metaphysical interests."[4]

Such subtle selection and canon formation, with their political and ideological implications, confront a resistant reader in the majority of western evaluations of Commonwealth writing. The following passage from Northrop Frye's "Across the River and Out of the Trees" is especially significant as it served as the theme for the 1984 conference of the Canadian Association of Commonwealth Languages and Literature Studies:

> In an 'instant world' of communication, there is no reason for cultural lag or for a difference between sophisticated writers in large centres and naive writers in smaller ones. A world like ours produces a single international style of which all existing literatures are regional developments. This international style is not a bag of rhetorical tricks but a way of seeing and thinking in a world controlled by uniform patterns of technology, and the regional development is a way of escaping from that uniformity. If we read, say, Wilson Harris's *Palace of the Peacock* and then Robert Kroetsch's *Badlands* one after the other, we find that there is no similarity between them, and that one story is steeped in Guyana and the other in Alberta. But certain structural similarities, such as the fold over in time, indicate that they are both products of much the same phase of cultural development.[5]

The tone of the passage is very disturbing to me, a critic of new Commonwealth origins. For one thing, Frye seems to equate technological advance with literary evolution. The phrase "cultural lag" suggests a rather condescending attitude towards the traditional indigenous literatures. Then, we are not informed as to the time this revolution in literature is supposed to have taken place. The causality is equally mysterious. Is the relatively new sophistication that Frye sees in the modern Third World literature a result of the new "way of seeing and thinking" that is supposed to have come with the "uniform patterns of technology"? Obviously, Frye wants it both ways. For if Frye had attributed the sophistication of the "naive writers" solely to the influence of the "sophisticated writers," one could have validly objected that the hinterland society may not necessarily be sophisticated enough for comprehending the imported "international style." In order to ward off that objection, Frye claims that the "uniform patterns of technology" have brought societies around the world to the same level. Thus, one can say that if there are structural affinities in writers across the nations, they occur automatically, because of the similarity of life patterns brought about by technology.

It is clear to me that Frye's mental contortions and contradictions lead up to the same "universalist" approach that Achebe was protesting against. Achebe, and many others, reject Frye's claim that "uniform patterns of technology" have created a uniform world. As this discussion of the practice and pronouncements of several Indian and African writers will show, they assert that life in the Third World is different from life in London, Paris and New York. And they claim that the writer who writes about these differences has to create new forms for articulating these differences. Thus, while Frye believes in readymade forms, or archetypes, a writer like Achebe believes that the local realities dictate their own structures.

However, western critics have been so busy proving the universality of texts that they have had no time for dealing with the specificity of these texts. I would go further and state that the universalist categories of criticism have no means of dealing with the specificity of a text except in terms of setting or backdrop. The universalist methodology, in its exaggerated focus on form and character, neglects referentiality and context, thereby failing to assign inventiveness to writers who structure their works on those principles. The universalist critic, armed with his readymade categories of narrative technique, symbolic patterns, motifs such as journey or quest, bildungsroman, pastoral, etc. overlooks the formal complexities that arise when a work openly or cryptically utilises the collectively shared knowledge and experiences of a society: experience of colonialism, legends of heroes and villains, deeply-held belief systems, rhetorical pronouncements of local elite such as politicians, businessmen and movie stars. The universalist critic's lack of interest in the context also means that the fiercely political confrontations in the works from the Third World are de-radicalized. The western critical response to J.P. Clark's *The Raft* is a good example of this appropriation. As R. N. Egudu shows in his article, "J.P. Clark's *The Raft:* The Tragedy of Economic Impotence," the western critics have totally overlooked Clark's emphasis on economic exploitation and read the play in existentialist terms, seeing it as an exploration of "the general plight of Man" set adrift in an indifferent universe.[6]

Such existentialist-universalist lamentations on "the human condition" can be heard over and over again in western literary criticism and the same habits of discourse are carried over to the discussion of works from the new Commonwealth. The following remarks by Haydn Moore Williams on Jhabvala's work constitute a good example of the functions the "universal" performs:

> Jhabvala constantly stresses the universality of India's problems. Though institutions like the arranged marriage are traditionally Indian, many of the problems of the characters of Jhabvala's new Delhi could also be set in New York or London. . . .She gains this univer-

13

sality the more easily by concentrating on personal, amorous and marital themes within an acutely vivid observation of urban Indian society in the second half of the twentieth century.[7]

In this kind of analysis, the "universal" masks the refusal to see the unfamiliar and, perhaps, the uncomfortable. It helps Williams select "personal, amorous and marital themes" as the ones worth bothering about because they are the ones that can be understood anywhere. Earlier in the article Williams had commented that the central subject of Jhabvala's novels is "the theme of isolation, rebellion and reconciliation, and the problems of expatriation and adaptation to a foreign culture."[8] Once again, it is clear that the themes important to Williams are related to the private lives of individuals that never get tangled with the broad socio-political conflicts. Also, the implication is that conflicts can be solved at the individual level through individual action or through growth in maturity.

While this sort of critical approach may be applicable to the works emanating from the European tradition, it is inadequate for judging the works by the writers from the new Commonwealth for the simple reason that it remains silent about institutional exploitation, caste and class domination, and economic and political neo-colonialism, issues which cannot be resolved at the individual level through a personal growth in maturity. These are the factors that make life in Nigeria or India different from life in London, New York and Paris, and cause they treat the lives of their characters not as isolated individuals going on actual or spiritual journeys and finding their own individual resolutions, but as individuals moulded, confronted, and interfered with by their social environment at every step in their lives.

The western critic, his sensibility trained by the forms of western literature in which the individual has long held the centre of the stage, is unable to do justice to those works from the new Commonwealth in which community life and larger socio-political issues are of central importance.[9] When the western critic applies the categories of character development, psychological verisimilitude, individual relationships such as love and marriage, and individual confrontation of problems of existence to these works, he performs an act of violence. A very good example of this kind of violence is the UNESCO English translation of the Bengali classic *Pather Panchali*. The translators, claiming that the "naive genius" of Bibhuti Bhusan Bandopadhyaya was not familiar with the requirements of the novel form, chopped off about seventy five pages from the text:

In spite of its episodic structure and its occasional abrupt transitions from one incident to another, it is emotionally coherent, and its narrative is integrated about the children in their village. Yet it would appearthat the author achieved this coherence, this dramatic unity, without fully realizing tht he had done so; for having brought the story to a point of climax he does not end, but continues with chapters which emotionally and dramatically belong to the sequel...

With these considerations in mind we have ended *Pather Panchali* with Opu looking out of the train window sobbing his goodbye to his sister, his home and his village.[10]

One can only hope that no other works from the Third World have been mangled in this arbitrary, ethnocentric fashion. However, what the translators consider to be "episodic," "abrupt,"and "anticlimactic" seems so only if we think that the novel's main preoccupation is a character named Opu. The fact that the writer did not think so is ascertained by his title which refers to an oral art form of Bengal. The writer's choice to structure his work in the loose episodic manner of a *Panchali,* and to adopt the narrative persona of a *Panchali* singer is motivated by his need to go beyond the novelistic conventions of the west which have no provisions for addressing a group audience. What Bandopadhyaya wanted most was to portray a vanishing mode of life and when he chose a form which was also vanishing, he further intensified the sense of loss he wanted his readers familiar with the *Panchali* and its itinerant singers to feel. If we assume that the village of Nishchindipur, and not Opu, is the focus of the novel, we will come to appreciate the relevance of the section the UNESCO edition purged out. The last section describes the life of Opu's family in the city and how the city finally destroys the family. The novel's conclusion with the *Panchali* singer-narrator's sardonic comments on Opu's intense longing to go back to Nishchindipur has an inevitability that is quite obvious to the reader familiar with the indigenous form employed by the novelist.

As works like *Pather Panchali*, Prem Chand's *Godan*, Raja Rao's *Kanthapura,* and Salman Rushdie's *Midnight's Children* show, the Indian novelist often creates forms which are markedly different from the fiction which is structured around a central hero figure. All of these novels are crowded with characters who may be considered extraneous if one went by the conventions of a main plot and central characters. However, if one chose to read these novels as explorations of community life and its historic transformations, every thing seems to fall in its place. Instead of drawing Jamesian "portraits"of sensitive

15

It was an interesting revelation for me to read Chinua Achebe's claim that his contribution to the novel form was his "emphasis on the community, as opposed to the individual."[12] He reinforced my own conclusion that the individual centred forms of western literature did not display that richness of community life I had experienced in the works of major Indian and African novelists. His statement supported my belief that the decentring of the individual protagonist was the main difference between the western and Indian and African novel and that this decentring was related to our different notions about the individual.

Raymond Williams has commented that the disappearance of a recognisable social community has been the bane of the English novel and that the great works of nineteenth and early twentieth century are mournings for that lost community life. Rather than attempting to recreate a community, the novelists, Williams says, surrendered to the forces that were fragmenting it. Interestingly enough, what Williams would like to see in the English novel is quite similar to what does happen in the novels of writers like Achebe, Ngugi, Raja Rao and Rushdie:

> Not selected persons, not persons composed in a single life's trajectory or     around an idea or a theme; but there in the way neighbours are, friends are, the people we work with are. . . .
> And it is one of the paradoxes of developed individualism that in a later mode this is never really so; never so for others.[13]

I believe that the conventions of the individual centred forms make it possible for the western novelists to escape from directly confronting the burning social issues of their times. Issues such as the enclosure movement and the uprooting of rural population, industrial unrest, Chartism, colonization, and women's rights got treated only as adjuncts to the main plot that inevitably concerned itself with a man-woman relationship. In a recent feminist study called *Victims of Convention,* Jean E. Kennard has proposed something similar. She believes that a large number of Victorian as well as modern novelists have been unable to explore women's problems because they felt compelled to structure their novels according to the two suitor convention whereby a young woman is educated by the process of having to choose between two male suitors: one good and intelligent and the other evil.[14] While one may not totally agree with her diagnosis, the fact remains that the triangle has been a staple device in the western novel. The group-based western novels such as George Gissing's *The Odd Women* and Marilyn French's *The Women's Room* are an exception to this norm.

The writers in the new Commonwealth countries have had to reject the individual-centred novel as it does not reflect the important role of kinship relationships in the cultures of their countries. The custom of arranged marriage, for example, makes it virtually impossible for the Indian novelist to use the great theme of courtship and marriage, unless in a parodic way. As R.K. Narayan says, "The eternal triangle, such a standby for the western writer, is worthless as a theme for an Indian, our social circumstances not providing adequate facilities for the eternal triangle."[15] The novelist, then, has to construct new structures which will articulate the indigenous reality. These structures have to be different because the Indian or African experience of selfhood is different. For example, while western literature and philosophy have emphasized the primacy of the individual, the Indian literature and tradition have laid emphasis on the primacy of the family and the community. In the Indian context, the well-being of the individual is often tied to the well-being of the larger group to which he or she belongs.

The new Commonwealth novelists, then, have had to build structures which allow them to capture the spider-web of relationships which constitute community life in the developing countries. These structures may seem loose or episodic to the western critic, yet they have a coherence if judged in accordance with the forms of experience they set out to explore. These structures are political choices on the part of the new Commonwealth writers, a declaration that the metropolitan forms do not fit their needs. However, the innovations and experimentations of these writers have often gone unnoticed. Their use of parabolic structures, indigenous story telling conventions, folk tales, parodies of western and indigenous forms and rituals have not attracted adequate attention due to the critics' obsession with western categories. As J.P. Clark complained, the Third World writers are discussed as though they did not have "two hands"— one European and one homegrown — but only one.[16]

Contrary to the assertions of the liberal humanist critics, literary appreciation as well as literary production are culture based and no universal criteria can be worked out that will apply regardless of cultural differences. It is not possible to accept that the quest, the Jungian journey to the underworld, the individual's growth from ignorance to knowledge, etc. are "universal" archetypes. These are the forms created by a civilization whose physical frontiers have continually expanded during the last four centuries. For example, instead of the quest, the main motif of the Indian epics is exile. The characters of *The Ramayana* and *The Mahabharata* go to the forest against their will, in obedience to the command of the parents in the first one and as punishment for having lost at gambling in the second. Similarly, in Achebe's *Things Fall Apart*, exile from his tribal village is the greatest misfortune that befalls Okonkwo, second only to the disruption of the tribal pattern of life by the arrival of the coloniser.

The journey is a form suitable to the outsider and that is the way Conrad and Patrick White have used it in *Heart of Darkness* and *A Fringe of Leaves*. However, if one wants to explore the destruction of communities, as it appears to an insider, the quest will not do. However, our reverence for metropolitan opinions is so great that we cannot see without the lenses provided by our western training. In a paper on Arun Kolatkar's *Jejuri*, S.K. Desai comments on the "Westernized critical sensibility of Indian critics who have been quick to find in *Jejuri* a characteristic quest-poem or an odyssey-spiritual or anti-spiritual."[17] Similarly, Meenakshi Mukherjee, in a paper entitled "Macaulay's Imperishable Empire," laments the Indian critics' inability to think on their own. Their slavish attitude, she says, "makes it possible for a string of quotations from the latest western critics and a recitation of the current western literary jargon to be called literary criticism."[18]

Desai pleads for what he calls "cultural inwardness." He wants the western critics to familiarize themselves with the culture before they comment on its literature. He also finds fault with the lack of awareness on the part of western critics about what is being said about indigenous literary works by the native critics and readers.

However, though Commonwealth literature is now taught in several Canadian universities, few of them subscribe to Indian or African journals. I feel that the majority of the western critics are too simplistic in their response to the works of the new Commonwealth because they haven't bothered to familiarize themselves with the cultures from which these works have sprung. Therefore, they are unable to see these literary works in their relationship with the other discourses that go on in the society which produced them. As Fredric Jameson suggests, cultural artifacts have a "relational place in a dialogical system,"[19] and the work of the critic should be to bring out their relational nature. For example, literary works often use mythic structures, quotations of political, religious and business leaders, folk and scriptural wisdom, collectively revered cultural attitudes, and past literary works as sub-texts. The western critics, however, remain stone-deaf to these nuances which make all the difference in interpretation. Instead, they concentrate on the characters and events and "universalize" them. Take, for example, these remarks of S.C. Harrex on R.K. Narayan:

> Narayan's world abounds with images of turbulence, with 'harass-ments and distractions' and labyrinthine approaches to human rela-tionships. Man is contantly harassed by officialdom, red tape, bu-reaucracy: by the aggressive trigger-happy type . . ., or the supercili-ous western-educated enemy of tradition, or even the child armed with a catapult and sadistic urge.[20]

"Man" here stands for the whole of humanity, obviously. The word obscures from the user, as well as the reader, the divisions in a society. "Man is constantly harassed by officialdom" glosses over the fact that officialdom is quite selective in its behaviour. Nor does such identificatory terminology identify the causes of things and actions. They seem to happen mysteriously and for no apparent reason.

The "universalists" forget the relational place that Jameson was talking about. They forget that literary works are polemical, and that their polemicity can only be understood by taking their context into account. The "universalists" ignore these considerations when they talk about "Man." As far as critical responses to Indo-Anglian literature are concerned, for example, everything boils down to cliches such as western rationality and eastern spirituality. Thus, Kamala Markandaya's *A Silence of Desire* is reduced to a schematic reconciliation of the east west conflict in the Indian society. In such critiques, Dandekar stands for the western rational attitudes while his wife, Sarojini, symbolizes the spiritual east. [21] However, I see Dandekar as an individual caught in a great chain of hierarchy, oppressing those beneath him and oppressed by the ones above him. The hierarchy is symbolised by the eight-story tenement building Dandekar lives in and his progress in the hierarchy is traced through his gradual moves from the topmost floor to the ground floor. As a clerk, he epitomises India's lower middle-class, domineering with those below and submissive in front of the ones above. That this hierarchical nature of his relationships is the main issue of the novel becomes evident when Dandekar, after having been warned by his new superior, wonders whether he has not related to Sarojini as a boss all their married life. His symbolic value as a representative of the western way of life is further undercut by his fear of western films and the western notions of marriage. Dandekar does not want the hierarchical nature of his marriage to change and is frightened by what he sees as his wife's yearning for independence.

A *Silence of Desire* is much more than an abstract, mental anguish over the clash between western rationality and eastern spirituality, so-called. It is a concrete exploration of the realities of lower middle-class Indian life at the bureaucratic, matrimonial and economic levels. To restrict the novel to a simple theorem of east meets west is to trivialize it.

Such trivialization will continue to occur until the foreign critic acquires "cultural inwardness." To ignore the social context, i.e., the writer's dialogical relationship with his society, and to superimpose categories that claim to be beyond the restraints of specificity is to falsify and deradicalize the literary works of the new Commonwealth. In the neo-colonial situation, when the dictates of the metropolis determine what will be said, thought, written and read in the peripheries, we from the new Commonwealth face the danger of becoming alienated from our own realities. As C.D. Narsimaiyah says, our own critical faculties have been reduced to "catching up with other people's yesterdays."[22] Given the imperatives of present day imperialistic world order, the western critic must ask himself if he is not, per chance, playing the role of a cultural imperialist when he resorts to the "universalist" criteria.

## NOTES

[1] Chinua Achebe, "Thoughts on the African Novel," *Exile and Tradition: Studies in African and Caribbean Literature,* ed. Rowland Smith (New York: Africana Publishing Company, Dalhousie University Press, 1978), p. 4.

[2] Victor Ramraj, "V. S. Naipaul: The Irrelevance of Nationalism," *World Literature Written in English,* 23:1 (1984), 195.

[3] Ibid, 187.

[4] Helen Tiffin, "Commonwealth Literature and Comparative Methodology," *World Literature Written in English,* 23:1 (1984), 28.

[5] Northrop Frye, "Across the River and Out of the Trees," *Divisions on a Ground: Essays on Canadian Culture* (Toronto: Anansi, 1982), pp. 31-2.

[6] R.N. Egudu, "J.P. Clark's *The Raft:* The Tragedy of Economic Impotence," *World Literature Written in English,* 15:2 (1976), 297-304.

[7] Haydn Moore Williams, "Strangers in a Backward Place: Modern India in the Fiction of Ruth Prawer Jhabvala," *Journal of Commonwealth Literature,* 6:1 (1971), 63.

[8] Williams, p. 54.

[9] The following comments of Achebe are quite apropos here: "the other day one of them spoke of the great African novel yet to be written. He said the trouble with what we have written so far, is that it has concentrated too much on society and not sufficiently on individual characters and as a result it has lacked 'true' aesthetic proportions. I wondered when this *truth* became so self-evident and who decided that (unlike the other self-evident truth) this one should apply to black as well as white." Achebe, "Where Angels Fear to Tread," *African Writers on African Writing,* ed. G.D. Killam (London: Heinemann, 1973), p. 6.

[10] T.W. Clark, introduction, *Pather Panchali: Song of the Road,* by Bibhutibhushan Banerji (London: George Allen and Unwin, 1968), pp. 16, 15.

[11] I believe that we in the Third World have a hard time with the concept that an individual can either single-handedly change his destiny or is entirely responsible for what happens to him. I cannot forget that the life of my family was inexorably changed by the creation of Pakistan.

[12] Interview with P.A. Egejuru, *Towards African Literary Independence: A Dialogue with Contemporary African Writers* (Westport, Conn: Greenwood Press, 1980), p. 106.

[13] Raymond Williams, *The English Novel: From Dickens to Lawrence* (Frogmore: Paladin, 1974), p. 143.

[14] Jean E. Kennard, *Victims of Convention* (Hamden, Conn: Archon Books, 1978).

[15] R.K Narayan, "English in India," *Commonwealth Literature: Unity and Diversity in a Common Culture,* ed. John Press (London: Heinemann, 1965), p. 123.

[16] J.P. Clark, quoted in Abiola Irele, *The African Experience in Literature and Ideology* (London: Heinemann, 1981), p. 36.

[17] S.K. Desai, "Arun Kolatkar's *Jejuri:* A House of God," *Literary Criterion,* 15:1 (1980), 48.

[18] Meenakshi Mukherjee, "Macaulay's Imperishable Empire," *Literary Criterion,* 17:1 (1982), 38.

[19] Frederic Jameson, *The Political Unconscious: Narrative as a Socially Symbolic Act* (Ithaca, N.Y.: Cornell U Press, 1981), p. 85.

[20] S.C. Harrex, "R.K. Narayan: Some Miscellaneous Writings," *Journal of Commonwealth Literature,* 13:1 (1978), 71.

[21] S.C. Harrex, "A Sense of Identity: The Novels of Kamala Markandaya," *Journal of Commonwealth Literaute,* 6:1 (1971), 65, 67. Meena Shirwadkar in her *Images of Woman in the Indo-Anglian Novel* (n.p.; Sterling Publishers, 1979) notes that several male Indian critics have pigeonholed the novel in the same way.

[22] C.D. Narsimaiyah, quoted in Mukherjee, 38.

# Ideology in the Classroom: A Case Study in the Teaching of English Literature in Canadian Universities

This paper was written in order to articulate the sense of personal anguish and alienation I feel as a teacher of literature whose sex, race and birth in a newly independent Asian country set her constantly at odds with the consensus that appears to reign in the departments of English across Canadian universities. The terms of this consensus, it seems to me, are not so very different from the ones prevailing in American universities as demonstrated, for example, by Richard Ohmann in his *English in America.*

Generally speaking, we, the Canadian university teachers of English, do not consider issues of the classroom worth critical scrutiny. Indeed, there is hardly any connection between our pedagogy and our scholarly research. A new teacher, looking for effective teaching strategies, will discover to her/his utter dismay that no amount of reading of scholarly publications will be of any help when facing a class of undergraduates. In fact, the two discourses — those of pedagogy and scholarly research — are diametrically opposed and woe betide the novice who uses the language of current scholarly discourse in the classroom.

As an outsider, it has never ceased to amaze me that Canadian literary scholars do not seem perturbed by this doublespeak. Not having the same skills myself, I gape with open mouth at my colleagues who switch so easily from one to another. Perhaps, blessed with what Keats called "Negative Capability," they are able to hold two completely contradictory systems of thought in suspension.

Edward Said, in his essay in the volume *The Politics of Interpretation,* says that the "mission of humanities" in contemporary American society is "to represent *noninterference* in the affairs of the everyday world."[1] He charges the American practitioners of humanities with concealing, atomising, depoliticising and mystifying the "unhumanistic process" that informs the *laissez faire* society of what he calls "Reaganism." The classroom experience I narrate in this paper concretized for me the ahistorical realm in which American and, yes, Canadian, university teachers of literature ply their trade.

What I have recounted here is not unique at all and I continue to come across student papers that share the innocence about history I describe in this paper. However, the particular experience was a watershed in my personal history since it allowed me, for the first time, to articulate to myself the lineaments of my disagreement with the dominant academic discourses.

The case study presented here is taken from 1983-84, when I was teaching at the University of Regina, Saskatchewan. The large part of teaching done at the Department of English of that university consists of English 100: Introduction to Literature. It is a complusory course whereby the professors of English supposedly infuse first year students with a love of literature. Since the aim of the course is to acquaint students with prominent literary genres, almost all teachers of the course use anthologies that contain short stories, poems and, at times, plays and novels as well. Quite often, the anthologies are American.

The short fiction anthology I used for my introductory English 100 class — I deliberately chose a Canadian one — includes a short story by Margaret Laurence entitled "The Perfume Sea."[2] This story, as I interpret it, underlines the economic and cultural domination of the Third World. However, even though I presented this interpretation of the story to my students in some detail, they did not even consider it when they wrote their essays. While the story had obviously appealed to them — almost 40 percent chose to write on it — they ignored the political meaning entirely.

I was thoroughly disappointed by my students' total disregard for local realities treated in the short story. Nevertheless, their papers did give me an understanding of how their education had allowed them to neutralize the subversive meanings implicit in a piece of good literature, such as the Laurence story.

The story, from my point of view, is quite forthright in its purpose. Its locale is Ghana on the eve of independence from British rule. The colonial administrators are leaving and this has caused financial difficulties for Mr. Archipelago and Doree who operate the only beauty parlour within a radius of one hundred miles around an unnamed small town. Though the equipment is antiquated, and the parlour operators not much to their liking, the ladies have put up with it for want of a better alternative.

With the white clientele gone, Mr. Archipelago and Doree have no customers left. The parlour lies empty for weeks until one day the crunch comes in the shape of their Ghanaian landlord, Mr. Tachie, demanding rent. Things, however, take an upturn when Mr. Archipelago learns that Mr. Tachie's daughter wants to look like a "city girl" and constantly pesters her father for money to buy shoes, clothes and make-up. Mr. Archipelago, in a flash of inspiration, discovers that Mercy Tachie is the new consumer to whom he can sell his "product": "Mr. Tachie, you are a bringer of miracles! . . . There it was, all the time, and we did not see it. We, even Doree, will make history — you will see" (221).

The claim about making history is repeated twice in the story and is significantly linked to the history made by Columbus. For Mr. Archipelago is very proud of the fact that he was born in Genoa, Columbus' home town. The unpleasant aspect of this act of making history is unmistakably spelled out: "He [Columbus] was once in West Africa, you know, as a young seaman, at one of the old slave-castles not far from here. And he also, came from Genoa" (217).

The symbolic significance of the parlour is made quite apparent from the detailed attention Laurence gives to its transformation. While the pre-independence sign had said:

ARCHIPELAGO
English-Style Barber
European Ladies' Hairdresser
(211)

The new sign says:

ARCHIPELAGO & DOREE
Barbershop
All-Beauty Salon
African Ladies A Speciality
(221)

With the help of a loan from Mr. Tachie, the proprietors install hair-straightening equipment and buy shades of make-up suitable for the African skin. However, though the African ladies show much interest from a distance, none of them enters the shop. Two weeks later, Mercy Tachie hesitantly walks into the salon "because if you are not having customers, he [Mr. Tachie] will never be getting his money from you" (222). Mercy undergoes a complete transformation in the salon and comes out looking like a "city girl," the kind she has seen in the *Drum* magazine.

Thus, Mr. Archipelago and Doree are "saved" by "an act of Mercy" (226). They have found a new role in the life of this newly independent country: to help the African bourgeoisie slavishly imitate the values of its former colonial masters.

These political overtones are reinforced by the overall poverty the story describes and the symbolic linking of the white salon operators with the only black merchant in town. The division between his daughter and other African women who go barefoot with babies on their backs further indicates the divisive nature of the European implant. Other indications of the writer's purpose are apparent from her caricature of Mr. Archipelago and Doree, a device which prevents emotional identification with them. The fact that both of them have no known national identities — both of them keep changing their stories — is also significant for it seems to say that, like Kurtz in *Heart of Darkness,* they represent the whole white civilization.

The story, thus, underplays the lives of individuals in order to emphasize these larger issues: the nature of colonialism as well as its aftermath when the native elite takes over without really changing the colonial institutions except for their names.

This, then, was the aspect of the story in which I was most interested, no doubt being from a former colony of the *Raj* myself. During class discussions, I asked the students about the symbolic significance of the hair straightening equipment, the change of names, the identification of Mr. Archipelago with Columbus, the *Drum* magazine, and the characters of Mr. Tachie and Mercy Tachie.

However, the students based their essays not on these aspects, but on how "believable" or "likeable" the two major characters in the story were, and how they found happiness in the end by accepting change. That is to say, the two characters were freed entirely from the restraints of the context, i.e. , the colonial situation, and evaluated solely on the basis of their emotional relationship with each other. The outer world of political turmoil, the scrupulously observed class system of the colonials, the contrasts between wealth and poverty, were non-existent in their papers. As one student put it, the conclusion of the story was "the perfect couple walking off into the sunset, each happy that they had found what had eluded both of them all their lives, companionship and privacy all rolled into one relationship." For another, they symbolized "the anxiety and hope of humanity," "the common
problem of facing or not facing reality."

I was astounded by my students' ability to close themselves off to the disturbing implications of my interpretation and devote their attention to expatiating upon "the anxiety and hope of humanity," and other such generalizations as change, people, values, reality etc. I realized that these generalizations were ideological. They enabled my students to efface the differences between British bureaucrats and British traders, between colonizing whites and colonized blacks, and between rich blacks and poor blacks. It enabled them to believe that all human beings faced dilemmas similar to the ones faced by the two main characters in the story.

Though, thanks to Kenneth Burke, I knew the rhetorical subterfuges which generalizations like "humanity" imply, the papers of my students made me painfully aware of their ideological purposes. I saw that they help us to translate the world in our own idiom by erasing the ambiguities and the unpleasant truths that lie in the crevices. They make us oblivious to the fact that society is not a homogeneous grouping but an assortment of groups where we belong to one particular set called "us" and the other set or sets we distinguish as "them".

The most painful revelation came when I recognized the source of my students' vocabulary. Their analysis, I realized, was in the time-honoured tradition of that variety of criticism which presents literary works as "universal." The test of a great work of literature, according to this tradition, is that despite its particularity, it speaks to all times and all people. As Brent Harold notes, "It is a rare discussion of literature, that does not depend heavily on the universal 'we' (meaning we human beings), on 'the human condition,' 'the plight of modern man,' 'absurd man' and other convenient abstractions which obscure from their users the specific social basis of their own thought. . . ."[3]

Thus, all conflict eliminated with the help of the universal "we," what do we have left but the "feelings" and "experiences" of individual characters? The questions in the anthologies reflect that. When they are not based on matters of technique— where one can short circuit such problems entirely — they ask students whether such and such character deserves our sympathy, or whether such and such a character undergoes change, or, in other words, an initiation. As Richard Ohmann comments:

> The student focuses on a character, on the poet's attitude, on the individual's struggle toward understanding — but rarely if ever, on the social forces that are revealed in every dramatic scene and almost every stretch of narration in fiction. Power, class, culture, social order and disorder — these staples of literature are quite excluded from consideration in the analytic tasks set for Advanced Placement candidates.[4]

Instead of facing up to the realities of "power, class, culture, social order and disorder," literary critics and editors of literature anthologies hide behind the universalist vocabulary that only mystifies the true nature of reality. For example, the editorial introduction to "The Perfume Sea" considers the story in terms of categories that are supposedly universal and eternal:

> Here is a crucial moment in human history seen from inside a beauty parlour and realized in terms of the 'permanent wave.' But while feminine vanity is presented as the only changeless element in a world of change, Mrs. Laurence, for all her lightness of touch, is not 'making fun' of her Africans or Europeans. In reading the story, probe for the deeper layers of human anxiety and hope beneath the comic surfaces.[5]

Though the importance of "a crucial moment in history" is acknowledged here, it is only to point out the supposedly changeless: that highly elusive thing called "feminine vanity." The term performs the function of achieving the desired identification between all white women and all black women, regardless of the barriers of race and class. The command to probe "the deeper layers of human anxiety and hope"— a command that my students took more seriously than their teacher's alternative interpretation — works to effectively eliminate consideration of disturbing social-political realities.

This process results in the promotion of what Ohmann calls the "prophylactic view of literature."[6] Even the most provocative literary work, when seen from such a perspective, is emptied of its subversive content. After such treatment, as Ohmann puts it, "It will not cause any trouble for the people who run schools or colleges, for the military-industrial complex, for anyone who holds power. It can only perpetuate the misery of those who don't."[7]

The editor-critic, thus, functions as the castrator. He makes sure that the young minds will not get any understanding of how our society actually functions and how literature plays a role in it. Instead of explaining these relationships, the editor-critics feed students on a vocabulary that pretends that human beings and their institutions have not changed a bit during the course of history, that they all face the same problems as human beings. Thus, another anthology used by several of my colleagues divides its subject-matter into four groups called "Innocence and Experience," "Conformity and Rebellion," "Love and Hate" and "The Presence of Death." The Preface justifies the classification thus: "The arrangement of the works in four thematic groups provides opportunities to explore diverse attitudes toward the same powerful human tendencies and experiences and to contrast formal treatment as well."[8]

The problem is that it is the editors' fiat that has decided what the "powerful human tendencies" are and how they should be treated. The introductions to the four sections talk about "the protagonist" and "tendencies" in a language that conveys to me that literature is about initiation and loss of innocence, about the lone rebel fighting against such authoritarian agencies as the state and society, about love and hate between men and women, and, about the inevitability of death. Literature, according to this line of thinking, is obviously not about the problems of oppression and injustice, about how to create a just society, about how to understand one's situation in society and to do something about it. Literature does not speak about people as social beings, as members of political or social alliances that they have voluntarily chosen.

I would not like to act naive and ask, like Barbara Kessel: "Why is it impossible for liberal critics to conceive of miserable, oppressed people freely choosing to struggle against their own oppression?"[9] It is because it is far more comfortable to hide behind a vocabulary which, on the one hand, overlooks one's own privileged position and, on the other, makes everyone look equally privileged. It creates, in the imagination of the user, a society "free, classless, urbane," by lifting the work of art from "bondage of history."[10] And if, my students, who come mainly from the privileged section of an overall affluent society, perform the same sleight-of-hand, why should I feel unduly disturbed.

After all, as Auden says, "Poetry makes nothing happen." The only thing is, what, then, am I doing in that classroom?

Terry Eagleton says that "explanation and interpretation 'come to an end,' . . . when we arrive at a certain interpretative logjam or sticking-place and recognize that we shall not get any further until we transform the practical forms of life in which our interpretations are inscribed."[11] He makes me realize that I can't fight a Quixotic battle in the classroom for historicity and politicization. In fact, I have at times been accused by some of my outraged students of "bringing politics into a literature class." In a similar vein, a very well-respected Canadian scholar in my field intimated to me that my research was "old-fashioned," i.e. "sociological," and if I wanted to consolidate my precarious foot-hold in academia, I should think about doing some "fashionable" research, i.e. "semiotics," "deconstruction," "feminism" etc. (I found it interesting that feminism to him was only another "fashion".)

My feeling is that the transformation of the practical forms of life which Eagleton speaks of is not around the corner in Canada. Those on the margin face an uphill task in terms of sheer physical and moral survival in the system. Once accepted, they face the prospect of being typecast as the "token black," or the "token ethnic," or the "token feminist." Their "diversion," then, becomes a nice variation in the vast edifice of cultural reproduction that goes on in departments of literature and literary journals.

Said talks about the need for a "fully articulated program of interference."[12] This paper is a partial attempt in that direction. I have hoped to generate a debate over issues that are very important to me as a teacher and a non-white woman from the Third World.

I am glad this paper has finally found an audience. It was submitted in an earlier version to the "Literature and Ideology" category of the annual conference of the Association of Canadian University Teachers of English (ACUTE) held at Guelph in 1984. While ACUTE may have turned down this submission for reasons other than ideological, what I found really disturbing was the total lack of attention to pedagogical issues in the conference programme. After all, the bulk of our jobs are provided by first year English courses and the communication strategies we adopt in our classrooms should be an important part of our discussions when we meet for our annual conference. For the responses of our students constitute an important mirror for our performance and our values. It does not behoove us as scholars to be oblivious to the social repercussions of our activities in the classroom.

If one looks at the 1984 ACUTE conference programme, one gets the impression that the only officially sanctioned valid response to literary works is structuralist-formalist. The following topics are representative of the kind of fare conference participants were treated to: "Sedulous Aping?: Redefining Parody Today," "John Webster's Jacobean Experiments in Dramatic Mimesis," "What Does It Mean to Imitate an Action?" "Whalley on Mimesis and Tragedy," "Interruption in *The Tempest*" and so on. Even the "Literature and Ideology" category was appropriated for formalistic preoccupations: the two papers in this section were entitled "Christianity as Ideology in Rudy Wiebe's *The Scorched-Wood People*" and "Dickens' Good Women: An Analysis of the Influence of Social Ideology on Literary Form."

Surely, literature is more than form? What about the questions regarding the ideology and social class of the writer, the role and ideology of the patrons and the disseminators of literature, the role of literature as a social institution and, finally, the role of teacher-critic of literature as a transmitter of the dominant social and cultural values? Have these questions no place in our professional deliberations?

# NOTES

[1] Edward Said, "Opponents, Audiences, Constituencies, and Communities," *The Politics of Interpretation* , ed. W.J.T. Mitchell, (Chicago: U of Chicago P, 1983), p. 28.

[2] Margaret Laurence, "The Perfume Sea," *In Search of Ourselves*, ed. Malcolm Ross and John Stevens, (n.p., J. M. Dent, 1967), p. 201-27. Hereafter all quotations from the story are cited by page number within the text.

[3] Brent Harold, 'Beyond Student-Centered Teaching: the Dialectical Materialist Form of a Literture Course," *College English* , 34 (November 1972), p. 210.

[4] Richard Ohmann, *English in America: A Radical View of the Profession* (New York, Oxford U P, 1976), p. 59-60.

[5] Ross and Stevens, *In Search of Ourselves,* p. 210.

[6] Ohmann, p. 63.

[7] Ohmann, p. 61.

[8] Richard Abcarian and Marvin Klotz, ed. *Literature: The Human Experience* (New York: St. Martin's Press 1973), p. xiii.

[9] Barbara Bailey Kessel, "Free, Classless and Urbane?" *College English* , 31 (March 1970) p. 539.

[10] Northrop Frye, *Anatomy of Criticism: Four Essays* (Princeton: Princeton UP, 1957), p. 347-8.

[11] Terry Eagleton, "Ineluctable Options," *The Politics of Interpretation,* p. 380.

[12] Said, *The Politics of Interpretation,* p. 31.

# The Poetry of Michael Ondaatje and Cyril Dabydeen: Two Responses to Otherness

A number of immigrant writers from the Third World are active on the Canadian literary scene. They have brought a refreshing diversity of subject-matter and style to a literary tradition that had been predominantly concerned with the two founding races of Canada. That homogeneity and consensus have been challenged by immigrant writers who often work as a disruptive force when they challenge the official image of a white Canada or when they direct their pen to issues such as discrimination, prejudice and racism.

While the number of Third World immigrant writers in Canada is impressively large, as I found when working on a bibliography of South Asian poets in Canada, not all of them get acknowledgement in terms of publication by a large house or critical attention from Canadian academics. Michael Ondaatje[1] is one of the very few South Asian poets to have been heard by the white audience. Not only have his works been published by better-known publishers, he has been the recipient of two Governor-General's awards as well as critical acclaim in a number of articles by established Canadian critics. His poems are included in every undergraduate anthology.

This paper examines Ondaatje's work in the context of that by Cyril Dabydeen,[2] another Third World immigrant writer from a somewhat similar background. Both Ondaatje and Dabydeen come from former British colonies: the former from Sri Lanka and the latter from Guyana. Both of them have published several collections of poetry and prose. However, unlike Ondaatje's, Dabydeen's books have come out of small presses and remain basically unavailable in public or university libraries. Though he has published in various Canadian journals and magazines and has given readings in Canada, and abroad, critical attention to Dabydeen's work has been nonexistent.

In examining Ondaatje's and Dabydeen's works together, I intend to probe the reasons for Ondaatje's success vis-a-vis the inability of Dabydeen and other Third World immigrant poets to be heard. It is proposed that Ondaatje's success has been won largely through a sacrifice of his regionality, his past and most importantly, his experience of otherness in Canada, matters that are the stuff of Dabydeen's poetry. It is only recently, after a writing career of over fifteen years, that Ondaatje has come out with an autobiographical account of Sri Lanka, but again, it is a book in which his relationship with his country of origin is highly problematic.

This absence of any reference in his major work to his past or to his otherness in terms of his racial and cultural heritage is very intriguing insofar as omissions in a writer's work are as meaningful as the givens. The significance of the omissions becomes clear when we examine their extent by comparing Ondaatje's work with that of the other Third World immigrant writers whose dominant theme is displacement. The questions that must be asked are: how has

Ondaatje managed to remain silent about his experience of displacement or otherness in Canada when it is generally known to be quite a traumatic experience? And, secondly, has this suppression affected his performance as a poet?

I have chosen to focus on Dabydeen's work in order, first, to assess the importance of the areas of experience omitted by Ondaatje and, second, to answer questions as to the aesthetic and political implications of the omissions.

In his review of Ondaatje's first book, *The Dainty Monsters*, Douglas Barbour gives an interesting interpretation of Ondaatje's otherness:

> He owes much of his orginality to his background, I think. The exotic imagery which crowds the pages of this book appears to stem from his childhood memories of Ceylon. His poems are jungel-lush . . . [3]

The *New Yorker* reviewer of *Running in the Family* seems to have a somewhat similar impression of what Sri Lanka constitutes of:

> It is a kind of travel book — eloquent, oblique, witty, full of light and feeling — that keeps spilling over into poetry, . . . into fiction, into slapstick and high-class adventure. But it is only partly about the heat and mountains and jungle of Ceylon. Rather, it concnentrates on the queer, wild, uncontrollable countries that Lalla and Mervyn turned their lives into.[4]

Just as India seems to evoke the image of the sacred cows wandering through the streets in the white man's mind, Sri Lanka seems to trigger the images of untamed nature.

The question, then, is whether Ondaatje's work contains more than "the heat and the mountains and jungle" of Sri Lanka that the white critics are unable to see in their ethnocentricism. For surely, Sri Lanka has more to it than the three things mentioned above. It consists of seven million human beings who ostensibly must have a culture and a world view unique to them.

Unfortunately enough, despite the publication of his recent book, *Running in the Family,* a book supposedly devoted to his search for roots, Ondaatje's work gives few indications of his Sri Lankan background. Ondaatje, coming from a Third World country with a colonial past, does not write about his otherness. Nor does he write about the otherness of the Canadian society for him. Intriguingly enough, there is no trauma of uprooting evident in his poetry; nor is there a need for redefinition in a new context: the subjects that preoccupy so many immigrant writers. One scours his poetry in vain for any cultural baggage he might have brought with him when he came to Canada. Also absent are memories of familiar places, people and things.

If one were looking for a cross-cultural experience, or, a yardstick against which the "Canadian" writing could be measured in order to isolate the factors that make up its Canadianness, one would be equally disappointed. For here we do not see any bouncing off of one tradition against another, as we see in writers like Salman Rushdie. We do not have any references to writers of Sri Lanka or other Third World countries that would alert us to other ways of perceiving the world.

Instead, what we have is a poetry of unmediated present. Ondaatje wants to catch hold of the passing moment without imposing any categories on it. The poem entitled "The gate in his head," ostensibly about Victor Coleman's poetry, gives us an indication of his poetic aims. The mind of the poet should try to approximate the immediacy of the felt response:

> My mind is pouring chaos
> in nets onto the page.
> A blind lover, don't know
> what I love till I write it out.
> And then from Gibson's your letter
> with a blurred photograph of a gull.
> Caught vision. The stunning bird
> an unclear stir.
>
> And that is all this writing should be then,
> The beautiful formed things caught at the wrong moment
> so they are shapeless, awkward
> moving to the clear.[5]

As in Wallace Stevens, a poet who appears in several of Ondaatje's poems, the reality is defined as chaotic and ever-shifting, a succession of random images and sensations. And the poet, whom Ondaatje defines as a spider, a fisherman, a murderer, is perpetually engaged in a Promethean attempt to trap this chaos without imposing fictional categories upon it.

Evidently, the poet in this version is so involved with the chaotic flux of reality that the past becomes irrelevant except for the pain it evokes in the poet for having passed away. Consequently, there is no history or memory; only a paranoid urge to catch hold of the passing moment. As a poem entitled "Billboards" tells us, the poet, or his persona, has a "virgin past" which is "disturb[ed]" and "invade[d]" by the present evidences of his wife's past:

My mind a carefully empty diary
till I hit the barrier reef
that was my wife —
. . .
Here was I trying to live
with a neutrality so great
I'd have nothing to think of,
just to sense
and kill it in the mind.

(*RJ*, pp. 13-4)

The poem, supposedly funny, accurately describes the ahistorical nature of Ondaatje's poetry. His experience is not a collage where past subtly intermingles with the present but is eternally fresh. As another poem called "Walking to Bellrock" tells us, "and you swim fast your feet off the silt of history." Describing an experience in the wilderness, the poem emphasizes the pressure of the present sensations that wipe out the past:

> ···· there is no history or philosophy or metaphor with us.
> The problem is the toughness of the Adidas shoe
> its three stripes gleaming like fish decoration.
> The story is Russell's arm waving out of the green of a field.[6]

This denial of history for the sensations of the present means that the poetic experience is always fragmented and anti-social. It cannot, consequently, carry the cargo of the poet's otherness. The past, of necessity, remains buried and unexploited, unable to give a sense of direction and coherence to the present which is continuously described as chaotic.

However, it is not just Ondaatje who suffers from amnesia. As Charles Altieri's *Enlarging the Temple* points out, the price of this freedom from history is "a loss of philosophical depth and resonance," and its symptoms can be seen, according to him, everywhere in postmodern poetry. The poets, constantly in search of "numinous moments," of "the energies manifest in acts of intense perception," are unable to take in the social areas of experience:

> [M]orally an aesthetics of presence cannot suffice, however one manipulates it, because one needs abstract intellectual and imaginative structures by which to judge the present and to pose alternatives to it. . . . For no matter how acute one's sensibility, no matter how attentive one is to numinous energies, it is impossible to write public poetry or make poetry speak meaningfully about pressing social concerns without a return to some notion of cultural models preserving ethical ideals or images of best selves.[7]

Taking his models from Wallace Stevens and other contemporary American and Canadian poets, Ondaatje, thus, is trapped by a style and a way of thinking that perforce have to deny life in society because it is caught in a vicious cycle. The poet as "connoisseur of chaos" facing the "overwhelmingly anarchic or chaotic" "reality",[8] then weaving his "nets" or "webs" to capture that reality, then realizing that the reality has slipped out or been distorted, is locked in a perpetual dualism beyond which his poetry cannot go. And since the exercise has been done to death, ever since Coleridge began it, it is beginning to get wearisome. As Frank Lentricchia puts it, this group of "connoisseurs of chaos" which includes such important modern writers as Wallace Stevens, W.B. Yeats, Robert Frost and such foremost critics as Frank Kermode, Paul de Man and Murray Kreiger, describes reality as "hostile," "violent," "black and utter chaos," and the poet as "an exemplary figure of courage and health" who confronts this chaos at the risk of self-destruction.[9] The posture, also adopted by Ondaatje as well as his critics, becomes quite comic for the reader when reiteratedin such high sounding terms:

> ... Ondaatje admires Bolden because the latter is an artist who has gone, for whatever reason, too far in his commitment to a demanding art. His sensibility was so compulsively responsive to the pressure of life's dynamism and confusion that in order to represent its complexities he took risks with his own sanity. In attempting to articulate aspects of this reality (both internal and external) Bolden went mad.[10]

To quote Lentricchia again, this heroic pose exudes "such self-congratulation about the plight of being a modern, such arrogance and such self-pity."[11]

However, one could probably put up with it, if a poet did not base his whole oeuvre around this apparently insoluble problem. Stevens and Ondaatje, unlike Yeats and Frost, do exactly that. Almost the whole of their writing is concerned with the idea of the artist facing the chaos. What Robert Lowell said of Stevens fits Ondaatje just as well: "His places are places visited on a vacation, his people are essences, and his passions are impressions. Many of his poems are written in a manner that is excessively playful, suave, careless and monotonous."[12] Of course, Ondaatje's critics find different words for the things Lowell is talking about. They call them irony, distance and control.

Both Stevens and Ondaatje demonstrate that art need not draw upon the outside world or the poet's own experiences. Thus, Stevens came to "write about arpeggios and pineapples rather than about racial tensions in Hartford or the practices of the insurance company he was vice-president of...."[13] Similarly, Ondaatje, instead of writing about the reality of Canadian life or his Sri Lankan past, chooses to write about the "tension between mind and chaos" and it drives the artist to certain death. Even when he chooses specific historical figures, they become subservient to his dominant theme of mind versus chaotic the way reality. Billy the Kid, according to Ondaatje's critics, is the artist as murderer who distorts reality in his effort to capture it in static forms. Buddy Bolden, on the other hand, is the artist as victim who is destroyed by his single-minded devotion to spontaneity in artistic creation.

Here art has become truly self-reflexive. Poems are made about the act of writing poems. Or about other artists in the act of creation. Time and space, lives of real men and women, countries and cultures are irrelevant here. The question of otherness does not even arise as otherness can be experienced only when the self is in company. Once again, Lentricchia's remarks are very helpful in understanding what is missing in this king of poetry.

> The counsel of self-consciousness in the aesthetist mode does not urge the uncovering and bringing to bear of alternative perspectives which in dialectical inter-play might offer constraints to the excesses and blindnesses of single-minded ideology. The counsel of aestheticized self-consciousness is, rather, paralysis and despair.
>
> . . . Somewhere along the line, however, we must ask ourselves hether this late version of aestheticism is sufficient protection against the claims — moral, social, political — that can be levied on the discourse of intellectuals, or, an easier question to answer, whether a tiny community of *literati,* cherishing the insulation offered by their brand of self-consciousness, has ever, can ever, or should ever want to make aestheticism operative in the world.
>
> . . . [T]he poetics of self-consciousness may not be much more, as Sartre suggests, than an apology for infantile behaviour which must be judged accordingly because it is not being attributed to the legitimately irresponsible — that is, to the insane, to the senile, to children.[14]

In other words, the metaphysical scarecrow of "chaos" has cut the poet off from his fellow men in the ordinary walks of life. When the poet sails "to that perfect edge/where there is no social fuel"(*RJ*, p. 70), and remains there, he is indulging in a self-willed isolation as well as Romantic posturing. To judge this work as a heroic gesture of defiance in the face of the universe, as Ondaatje's critics have done, becomes a bit exasperating since when we place this discourse in the company of other discourses, a sense of déjà vu is very hard to avoid.

What I have attempted to say here is that Ondaatje's masters in the art of poetry have led him away from an exploration of his own realities. The Romanticist line of poetry is essentially ahistorical as it sings only of the intensities of the present. These poets write in universals: of Man and of what is called "the human condition" and not of men and the conditions of men. That is, the poet does not see the conflicts and contradictions dividing men but sings of man in the abstract as though his life amounted to this one single act of confrontation with what he calls chaos. There are no cultural and historical determinants here. Man, wherever he may be, is the same everywhere. Thus Ondaatje goes around the world to hunt for his subjects. Billy the Kid, Buddy Bolden, Mrs. Fraser and his own father are all "connoisseurs of chaos" and not situated human beings operating in a certain space and under certain historical conditions.

"Universal" is a highly approbatory term in the arsenal of the western critic. It performs the magic trick of eradicating whatever may be troublesomely other. It creates a homogeneous world of brotherhood, but at the critic's own terms. Whatever he suffers from, he ascribes the same symptoms to us. The term, thus, is a convenient shorthand for a person who does not want to come to terms with the multiplicity and diversity of cultural modes as well as differences of race and class.

Roland Barthes, commenting on a photographic exhibition called *The Family of Man,* purportedly describing the unity of mankind around the world through such universalist categories as love and death, points out the hidden ideological stance in such laudatory attempts at universal brotherhood. The analogy of the family hides what Barthes calls "injustices":

> Whether or not the child is born with ease or difficulty, whether or not his birth causes suffering to his mother, whether or not such a type of future is open to him: this is what your Exhibition should be telling people, instead of an eternal lyricism of birth.[15]

The problems with the universalist poetic become evident if we examine Ondaatje's *the man with seven toes.* Here, all particularity has been sacrificed to make an archetype of Mrs. Fraser, a middle class white woman of the nineteenth century, the wife of the captain of a British ship bringing convicts to Australia. Her experience in the bush after the shipwreck becomes an exploration of "the borderline between form and formlessness, civilization and nature, the human and the natural and the conscious reasoning mind and the unconscious world of instinct."[16] "The poem," Solecki tells us elsewhere, "is the account of the confrontation with and gradual acceptance of the darker and more chaotic aspects of life which by the book's end are recognized as not only outside the self but within it as well."[17] That is, we are asked to make of Mrs. Fraser's life with the aborigines and the white convict a Jungian journey into the unconsious and forget about its political implications.

It seems to me highly unfair of both Ondaatje and Solecki that they trivialize Sidney Nolan's treatment of the theme, the Australian artist who inspired Ondaatje's work. While they use his name, as well as the quotations from a book on him, they don't tell us that Nolan sees Mrs. Fraser as a colonizer and presents the aborigines and the convict as victims of her class and not, as Ondaatje paints them, where they become rapists as well as embodiments of the irrational. Colin MacInnes' *Sidney Nolan,* the book that gave Ondaatje the idea for his own book, gives a highly political interpretation of the myth:

This 'betrayal' theme — in which the traitoress is portrayed naked in grotesque postures, and the stripes of her saviour's convict dress in skeletonic bars — is evidently one that preoccupies the artist since he returned to it again in 1957. . . . And basically, perhaps, is an allegory of the conflict between the European expatriates who explored and governed and 'squatted' on the land, and bullied and slew the prisoners and aborigines, but who never became the true Australians.[18]

In suppressing the political theme, in making Mrs. Fraser a Jungian quester, in stereotyping the aborigines as the primitive and irrational, Ondaatje takes sides with the colonizer. He needs to realize that history, even when delivered "point blank"[19] has a hidden ideological content which does not go away just by universalizing it. It is highly unfortunate that a poet originating in the Third World should be glamorizing the colonizers.

Raymond Williams in his *The Country and the City* shows how the Romantic landscape poetry turned a blind eye towards the people who worked in the landscape. Instead of showing the human beings in relations of production, what it shows is "a rural landscape emptied of rural labour and of labourers; a sylvan and watery prospect, with a hundred analogies in neopastoral painting and poetry, from which the facts of production had been banished: . . . inconvenient barns and mills cleared away out of sight . . . and this landscape seen from above, from the new elevated sites; the large windows, the terraces, the lawns; the cleared lines of vision; the expression of control and of command."[20] Ondaatje's *Running in the Family* is similarly elliptical. We are repeatedly given paradisical images of flower gardens, paddy fields, tea estates and forest reserves but no contemporary picture of Sri Lanka — which Ondaatje calls Ceylon — emerges. Williams' words on Trollope are equally applicable to Ondaatje's book: "What is seen is a social structure with pastoral trimmings. The agricultural poor are placed easily between the produce and the pleasures. And while this easy relationship holds, there is no moral problem of any consequence to disturb the smooth and recommending construction."[21] Reading *Running in the Family* one gets the impression that the other Sri Lankans — the fishermen, the tea estate pickers, the paddy planters — are only there as a backdrop to the drama of the Ondaatje family which is described in the analogy of Greek tragedy. We hear about the "race riots" because Ondaatje's uncle is directing an enquiry commission but we are not told what they are about. Ondaatje is similarly fuzzy about the student revolt in 1971 and its meaning. We are shown vignettes of people dancing in the moonlight to imported songs of the twenties. We hear about continuous traffic of people going to Oxford and Cambridge. We see Ondaatje's mother dancing in the style of Isadora Duncan, reading Tennyson's poetry and Shakespeare's plays. However, we hear about the independence only in parenthesis. We do not hear about Ondaatje's family's exploitative relationship to Sri Lanka. Their life style is described in generalist terms like "everyone" or "people," which might give the impression to the unwary reader that everyone in Sri Lanka lived like that. Ondaatje mentions Leonard Woolf's novel about Sri Lanka but glosses over the sordid realities created by centuries of colonial exploitation as well as the iniquities of plantation economy that Woolf's novel described so vividly.

Ondaatje's unwillingness or inability to place his family in a network of social relationships makes the book a collection of anecdotes which may or may not be funny depending on one's own place in the world. The reader who sees the Ondaatje family as belonging to the compradore class is put off by Ondaatje's sentimental tone and lack of perspective.

For me, the only redeeming feature of the book was the one stanza Ondaatje quotes from a poem of Lakdasa Wikkramasinha:

> Don't talk to me about Matisse . . .
> the European style of 1900, the tradition of the studio
> where the nude woman reclines forever
> on a sheet of blood
>
> Talk to me instead of the culture generally —
> how the murderers were sustained
> by the beauty robbed of savages: to our remote
> villages the painters came, and our white-washed
> mud-huts were splattered with gunfire.

Ondaatje admits with a disarming candidness that this poetry represents "The voices I didn't know."[22] To me, Ondaatje's ignorance of these voices of otherness is a good indication of what is wrong with poetry. Yeats said that one needed responsibility and allegiance to become a poet: "poetry needs a God, a cause, or a country."[23] Lacking all three, Ondaatje's poetry speaks of ironies of perception in a voice that always remains calm and controlled. It is a poetry that has turned a blind eye to the realities of here and now in favour of a jaded metaphysics that is ultimately spurious. His case is a sad example of cultural domination of the Third World intellectuals who cannot see their world without applying imported categories to it. And he is certainly not alone.

If we contrast Ondaatje's work with that of Dabydeen's, we come to see the importance of the areas that Ondaatje has blocked out. Instead of locking himself into the Romantic no man's land, "the edge/where there is no social fuel," Dabydeen, learning from Robert Lowell, Wilson Harris and Martin Carter — the poets he says he has been influenced by — situates the individual experience in a community. He sings of the history of his community rather than of the naked individual in converse with the universe. As a member of an identifiable community, he sings of the contradictions and conflicts of men, men in power relationships, men as pitted against each other as dominant or dominated others.

Dabydeen's poetry shows that while otherness is alienating and burdensome, it also provides a unique insight because of the double vision the "other" can claim to possess. What seems natural and self-evident to the well-adjusted member of a society, becomes highly problematic when seen from the eyes of an outsider. The outsider burrows under the suppressions of the dominant versions of history and myth and brings out their ambivalences and disjunctions. The other, thus, serves as a measuring rod against which a culture can take stock of itself. He serves as a mirror where a culture may see itself as others see it. For cultural traits are inconspicuous to the members of a culture who remain oblivious to the dangers of ethnocentricism. If nothing else, the outsider can make a culture self-conscious and that in itself is a great achievement.

Dabydeen's "Señorita" is a good example of what an outsider's dispassionate glance can reveal. Having had the privilege of going to school in Canada myself, the poem touches a raw nerve in me:

> This Señorita from the Dominican
> Republic flashes a smile;
> she tells me she has attended school
> in Canada, is interested in Lope de Vega
> and extols the Golden Age of Spain.
> I remind her of Pablo Neruda
> and Nicolas Guillen,
> both closer to her home.
> She still smiles, professes
> a dim acquaintance with the poetry
> of both, talks about water imagery
> in Neruda. I remind her about the latter's
> fire of love, the Cuban's revolutionary
> zeal. She's not impressed.
> She still smiles however.
>
> How about the poets
> of the Dominican Republic?
> She smiles once more. "Ah, do you
> not see I have been educated
> in Canada?" she protests innocently.

"Five million people there —
surely there must be poets!"
I exclaim in silent rage.
Once more the Señorita smiles —
as bewitching as a metaphor.[24]

The poem's inclusiveness seems an astounding achievement to me. Apart from attacking the apolitical and amoral stance of our English Departments, it also succeeds in showing, paradoxically enough, the political repercussions of this apolitical stance in the colonial situation. The formalist training the "Señorita" receives in Canada has effectively cut her off from her native tradition. It prevents her from responding to the revolutionary message of Neruda's poetry whose imagery she can discuss so glibly. No severer attack could have been made on the Third World intellectuals who so unashamedly live off the crumbs of western learning while remaining totally oblivious to their own heritage.

Ironically, Dabydeen's *This Planet Earth,* a collection full of poems as pungent as "Señorita," elicits a remark from the reviewer of *Canadian Literature* that echoes this poem's version of Canadian education: "Though less versatile and sure in its treatment, it shares with *Divinations* recurrent dualism, especially light/dark image patterns, a concern with the 'ephemeral, trivial,' with people who, monstrously closed in upon themselves, seek escape or transcendence."[25]

The truth of the poem's charge is self-evident. The critic has successfully neutralized the disturbing political context of the poems by using a universalist vocabulary full of abstractions and technicalities. He can only see "people" trapped in their self-made prisons whereas the poetry clearly assigns causes to their fate.

Another reviewer dismisses *Goatsong* because of its "obvious observations about poverty, love, and human cruelty."[26] It seems that until you become deliberately ambiguous and esoteric, the Canadian critic will not bother to take notice.

However, if Dabydeen's poetry seems obvious, it is because of the lessons he learnt from Lowell who wanted to write poems "as open and single-surfaced as a paragraph."[27] The simplicity of such poetry has been won the hard way. The austerity and bareness of Dabydeen's poetry, its sparing diction and natural syntax conceal a craftsmanship which is amazingly effective in conveying his perceptions of the tensions and contradictions of the Canadian society.

"Lady Icarus," a poem the reviewer found trite and sentimental, is a good example of Dabydeen's method. Dabydeen dislodges a highly charged western myth from its usual moorings to dislocate the reader. The myth becomes the carrier of a socio-political message for the first time:

Lady Icarus
"ordered deported — for the 5th time"

You fell, you
fell from seven
stories high
tempting gravity
from the Strathcona
hotel

not skyward
only landward

like a recalcitrant
angel, Maria,
all the way
          from Ecuador

you came, wanting
desperately to stay
in Canada
          so glorious
and free — defying
another deportation
order when suddenly
your rope

of sheets and blankets
broke
no sun now melting wax
your hold snaps
          as you plunge
to sudden death
we stand on guard for thee
Oh so glorious and free

O Canada   O Canada
          (*G*, p.16)

The myth and the national anthem provide an ironic structure to the poem. The fact that Maria has escaped the immigration authorities five times in the past equates her determination quite effectively with that of the protagonist of the myth. The phrase "so glorious/ and free" could apply to both Maria and Canada because of the syntax and makes the poem highly ambiguous in its accordance of a heroic status to Maria while being ironical about the anthem at the same time. The poem attacks the discrepancy between theory and practice and does it through a strikingly novel use of the Icarus myth. Further, though unlike Icarus, Maria is going downward when her rope breaks, her journey from Equador to Canada is truly upward. The poem hints at the mythic Canada that resides in the minds of many Third World would-be immigrants and a Canada, which, paradoxically, like the sun, eludes their grasp.

Instead of writing about the numinous moments of vision, Dabydeen persists in confronting the reader with facts of history which determine the direction of the present. However, the tone is not propagandistic and declamatory but intensely personal. Again, like Lowell, Dabydeen displays a knack of interjecting the intensely personal into the public and historic. "Fruit, of the earth," another favourite of mine, about a Guyanese family fallen on hard times, conveys a complex experience to the reader. While its lush imagery evokes the colours and tastes of the tropical fruit, the use of the past tense throughout the poem pulls against the images of plenty and speaks of a paradise already lost. The statement about the "balance of/payments" brings home the unjust deprivation the family has suffered. The poem successfully draws the contradictions of misery among plenty as well as subtly hinting at the problems faced by most Third World countries' economies. Also, the reader is forced to realize that the fruit this family has been deprived of, the title hinting a further irony through its Biblical echo, adorns the counters of our supermarkets. It seems miraculous to me that such a complex statement is made so cryptically.[28]

"Sir James Douglas: Father of British Columbia"[29] is a poem densely packed with the intersecting histories of Canada and Guyana and demonstrates the advantages an immigrant poet has through his access to two cultures. The poem is a meditation spurred by the poet's visit to Demerara, his birth place, but which also happens to be Sir James Douglas' birthplace. The poem fuses the public and the private and the national and the global without any straining. It insists on pointing out the common colonial past of Guyana and Canada and the fact that they were ruled by the same family of rulers. The poem is also a good indication of the aptness of the title Dabydeen has chosen for the collection. *This Planet Earth* places Canada in a global framework, tied in a web of relationships and impinging on the lives and destinies of people of the Third World. The title, though it seems to echo McLuhan's global village image, actually subverts the happy pastoral vision evoked by that phrase. For the relationships Dabydeen is talking about are exploitative, the relationships of the metropolis to the hinterland.

Dabydeen's poetry can be called a poetry of subversion. It continually attacks the romantic, tourist guide version of the tropics and uncovers the relationships of production. "Tourist Magazine" (*G*, p. 20), like Birney's "Sinaloa," contrasts the romance of the tourist paradise with the grim realities of hunger. "Ancestry" (*D*, p. 15), similarly, employs a nursery rhyme for ironic purposes:

> The moon throws
> light in the eyes
> of half-naked children
> A cow ambles along
> and jumps over the moon
> a sheep bleats in
> blakean innocence
> a song for master
> and dame while
> the little black boy
> strides doggedly
> along the caribbean
> lane

The short stanza speaks volumes about the constraints of class on our perceptions. Dabydeen insists that we realize that the sheep's song, and wool, are for the master and the dame. By making the little boy "black," Dabydeen turns the nursery rhyme into a colonial's protest while the insertion of "caribbean" before "lane" firmly situates the poem.

The moon-drenched landscape reminds the reader of Dabydeen's ironic twists. It is neither used for Romantic meditations nor as a backdrop for the personal pains and joys. Instead, it becomes a means of drawing in the troubled history of his country. The ironic usage of the language of the masters gives it the satiric edge. Again, the poem pinpoints the meaning of the collection's overall title, *Distances.* The distances are racial, historical, economic as well as spatial.

Dabydeen's strong sense of history transforms everyday objects of our world into strangely disturbing symbols. Molasses, for example, is a word that an ordinary reader associates with grandma's wholesome cooking. For the Guyanese poet, however, the word evokes painful memories of the colonial era:

> . . . I am astride a dolphined ship,
> My muse gliding along, each hump-backed
> Wave carrying me farther away
>> Middle passage again,

45

I breathe sugar, molasses my skin
The heat increasing in the Shangrila
Of a new sun —
A town's life burgeoning. Shapes and shacks
I am the hovel of despair
A crow flying low
Circles  the tenement life
Far from Bombay.[30]

Dabydeen's poetry is full of references to the sugarcanes as well as other products of the plantation economy. The "indentured" labourers who were brought to work in the plantations recur frequently in Dabydeen's poetry as ancestral memories. The poem "Letter,"describing the common immigrant experience of pain and unease when one does not hear from home, gains tremendously in depth and resonance by referring to the "indentured." The reference pulls in an entire chapter of colonial history which uprooted people from their homes so that the plantation owners could get cheap labour.

You have not written
these past weeks:
a mail strike perhaps.

I do not give up
easily: remembering
old words

like salted cod
in the penury of taste.
And the dim slaves

with their leather
tongues: the indentured
also grew accustomed


to neglect
in the humid heat.

(G, *p.* 5)

Dabydeen's achievement, I believe, resides in making the condition of otherness accessible to the sympathetic outsider. In "Letter," for example, the grounding of the historical in the immigrant's immediate experience in Canada, and the fortunate choice of an image like "salted cod" which will also appeal to the Canadian sensibility make sure that the past suffering of the "dim slaves" will become real to a reader situated outside that history.

Another effective device is the use of names of historical personages and prominent Third World personalities. Jose Marti and Che Guevara rub shoulders with Amour de Cosmos and Sir Walter Raleigh. Their juxtaposition hints at contradictions and conflicts the colonizer's version of history overlooks. Again, the unsituated reader is lured by the names he might have come across in Canadian history books. However, the poetry shows us their unfamiliar side.

Naming provides a resonance and complexity that works against the apparently transparent texture of the poem. Though it is true that the unfamiliar names make the poems obscure at times, researching them is an added pleasure for a reader who wants to learn about the world.

The poem "New Life"(*TPE*, p. 64), referring to the poet's life in Canada, makes the statement that the poet's self is "mudbound in memory". This powerful image encapsulates for me the entirety of the immigrant experience in Canada: the past is not just the ethnic costume that one wears on ceremonial occasions but a visible badge that cannot be got rid of easily. More than that, the physical sensation of walking in mud sodden shoes vividly captures the weight of the past the immigrant mind carries. The mud imagery also makes clear why Dabydeen's poetry sticks to the ground instead of taking off to the border realms.

The absence of the Romantic mode and its universalist rhetoric are thus, deliberate. Like Lowell, Dabydeen seems to feel that "our world lies all before us and nowhere else."[31] A statement by Sartre is quite relevant to my point here. Metaphysics, he says will remain "the privilege of an Aryan ruling class" for the time being as "one must be quite sure of one's rights in society to be able to concern oneself with the fate of man in the universe."[32]

The statement quite bluntly points out why the dominant mode of western poetry remains metaphysical and why it has such limited usefulness for a poet so conscious of his alienation and his colonial situation as Dabydeen. His allegiance, as the collections amply prove, is with "those without power." He declares himself to be a "metaphysical socialist," a "humanist" concerned about the "improvement of man's lot in society." He ascribes this position to the fact of having grown up in a "semi-ghetto in Guyana."As a result, "the human condition" to him means "real suffering, real joy,"[33] and not just the existentialist nausea in the face of so-called "chaos."

The universalist vocabulary, in its rhetoric of identification and its blurring out of particularities seems to me the crux of the matter. The universalist lives in an ahistorical, timeless world where the present simply repeats the cycle. For Ondaatje, whom I take to be a universalist, "theme," i.e., particularities of time and space, is "a minor part of the poem. If you read a love poem, well obviously there will be nothing new in a love poem — it's the way it's said and it's the *way* it's said that makes it suddenly hit you."[34] However, as Barthes shows, it is the situation in which the love making is carried out which is important as opposed to the blurring generality that love is part of a universalist human nature. There are people who make love on their pavement home in Calcutta and then there are people who make love surrounded by candlelight and elegant furniture.

"The principal function of the universal in a colonial situaton," Arnold Rampersad says, "is to destroy, defame, or defuse political analysis."[35] The poet who chooses to speak to all men, I feel, is only indulging in a fiction. He has simply refused to address himself to the particular needs of his community. The otherness is a fact of life and the universalist, by overriding it, is simply in retreat from the questions of ideology, power, race and class. It is only history which makes one confront these questions. And since history involves naming: injustices, ancestors, acts of friendship and acts of enmity, it automatically calls for the poetry of otherness. Dabydeen's poetry is an encounter with history and hence with his otherness.

[1] Ondaatje, *The Dainty Monsters* (1967), *the man with seven toes* (1969), *The Collected Works of Billy the Kid: Left Handed Poems* (1970), *Rat Jelly* (1973), *Coming Through Slaughter* (1976), *There's a Trick with a Knife I am Learning to Do: Poems 1963 to 1978* (1979), *Running in the Family* (1982)

[2] Dabydeen, *Distances* (1977), *Goatsong* (1977), *Heart's Frame* (1979), *This Planet Earth* (1979), *Still Close to the Islands* (1980), *Elephants Make Good Step Stepladders* (1982).

[3] Douglas Barbour, "Controlling the Jungle," *Canadian Literature*, 36 (Spring 1968), 86.

[4] Whitney Balliett, *The New Yorker*, Dec. 27, 1982, p. 76.

[5] Michael Ondaatje, *Rat Jelly* (Toronto: The Coach House Press, 1973), p. 62. Hereafter the collection is cited as *RJ* .

[6] Ondaatje, "Walking to Bellrock," *Capilano Review*, 7 (Spring 1975), 126.

[7] Charles Altieri, *Enlarging the Temple: New Directions in American Poetry during the 1960s* (Lewisburg: Bucknell UP, 1979) pp. 18, 20.

[8] Sam Solecki, "Nets and Chaos: The Poetry of Michael Ondaatje," in *Brave New Words,* ed. Jack David (n.p.: Black Moss Press, 1979), p. 24.

[9] Frank Lentricchia, *After the New Criticism* (Chicago: The U of Chicago P, 1980), pp. 53, 55.

[10] Solecki, "Nets and Chaos: The Poetry of Michael Ondaatje," p. 47.

[11] Lentricchia, p. 54.

[12] Robert Lowell, "Imagination and Reality," a review of *Transport to Summer, Nation, April 5,* 1947; rpt. in *Wallace Stevens,* Penguin Critical Anthologies (Harmondsworth: Penguin Books, 1972), p. 155.

[13] Meredith Tax, "Introductory: Culture is not Neutral, Whom Does it Serve?" in *Radical Perspectives in the Arts,* ed. Lee Baxandall (Harmondsworth: Penguin Books, 1972), p. 16.

[14] Lentricchia, pp. 57-8.

[15] Roland Barthes, *Mythologies,* trans. Annette Lavers (New York: Hill and Wang, 1972), pp. 100-2.

[16] Sam Solecki, "Point Blank: Narrative in Michael Ondaatje's 'the man with seven toes',"*Canadian Poetry,* 6 (Spring/Summer 1980), 14.

[17] Solecki, "Nets and Chaos: the Poetry of Michael Ondaatje", p. 29.

[18] Colin MacInnes in Kenneth Clark et al, *Sidney Nolan* (n.p.: Thames and Hudson, 1961) p 22.

[19] Ondaatje, 'O'Hagan's Rough Edged Chronicle", Canadian Literature, 61 (Summer 1974), 24.

[20] Raymond Williams, *The Country and the City* (1973: rpt. Frogmore, Herts: Paladin, 1974), p. 155.

[21] Ibid., p. 214.

[22] Ondaatje, *Running in the Family* (Toronto: McClelland and Stewart, 1982), pp. 85-6.

[23] Quoted by Thomas R. Whitaker, "Poet of Anglo-Ireland,"*Modern Poetry: Essays in Criticism,* ed. John Hollander (New York: Oxford UP 1968), p. 413.

[24] Dabydeen, *Goatsong* (Ottawa: Mosaic Press, 1977), p. 28. Hereafter cited as *G.*

[25] Michael Hurley, *Canadian Literature,* 89 (Summer, 1981), p. 167.

[26] Ron Miles, *Canadian Literature,* 81 (Summer, 1979), p 138.

[27] Quoted by Eric Homberger, *The Art of the Real: Poetry in England and America since 1939* (London: Dent, 1977), p. 142.

[28] Dabydeen, *Distances* (n.p.: Fiddlehead, 1977), p. 10. Hereafter cited as *D.*

[29] Dabydeen, *This Planet Earth* (Ottawa: Borealis Press, 1979), pp. 41-2. cited as *TPE.*

[30] Dabydeen, *Elephants Make Good Stepladders* (London, Ont.: Third Eye,

1982), p. 48.

[31] Quoted by Altieri, *Enlarging the Temple,* p. 63.

[32] Quoted by M. Adereth, *Commitment in Modern French Literature: Politics and Society in Peguy, Aragon, and Sartre* (New York: Schocken Books, 1968), p. 19.

[33] Dabydeen, letter to the author.

[34] Ondaatje, "Moving to the Clear," an interview with Jon Pearce in *Twelve Voices: Interviews With Canadian Poets* (Ottawa: Borealis Press, 1980), p. 135.

[35] Arnold Rampersad, "The Universal and the Particular in Afro-American Poetry,"*CLA Journal,* 25 (September, 1981), p. 8.

# South Asian Poetry in Canada:
## In Search of a Place

In their introduction to a special issue of *Canadian Ethnic Studies* devoted to the theme of "Ethnicity and Canadian Literature," the editors, commenting on the "predominantly Anglo-Gaelic or French character" of the official view of Canadian literature, ask, "where are the fictional remembrances of the Chinese, the Japanese, the Greeks, the Finns, the Ukrainians, to name only a few?"[1] Several publishing events in recent years suggest the development of a real awareness in the intellectual circles of the pluralistic nature of Canadian society. In addition to the *Canadian Ethnic Studies* special issue, *Canadian Literature* brought out a special issue on Caribbean writers in Canada in winter 1982, while the *Journal of Canadian Studies* published an issue on multiculturalism in spring 1982. Perhaps intellectual acts such as these will result in a rewriting of Canadian literary and cultural history — a longer rejoinder to E.J. Pratt's "Towards the last Spike" than F.R. Scott's short reprimand to Pratt for overlooking the role of the Chinese workers in building the transcontinental railroad.

A notable additon to this multicultural Canadian literature is the work of writers of South Asian origin.[2] These writers deserve to be acknowledged on the strength of numbers alone. Indeed, the number of South Asian writers active on the Canadian literary scene is quite astounding given the fact that South Asians, who are relatively new to Canada, account for less than one percent of the country's population. A very encouraging sign of the vitality of South Asian writing in Canada is the publication of journals like *The Toronto South Asian Review* , which provide a forum for South Asian creative and critical writing. Aside from Michael Ondaatje, however, only one other writer, Bharati Mukherjee, has gained much attention in Canada as a creative writer.[3]

In this paper I intend to comment on the work of South Asian poets in Canada. Apart from Ondaatje, who needs no introduction, Himani Bannerji, Krisantha Sri Bhaggiyadatta, Rienzi Crusz, Cyril Dabydeen, M. Lakshmi Gill, Réshard Gool, Arnold Itwaru, Surjeet Kalsey, Suniti Namjoshi, S. Padmanab, Uma Parameswaran and Asoka Weerasinghe have all had at least one collection of their poems published.[4]

While these poets admittedly come from different parts of the globe — for example, Guyana, India, the Philippines and Sri Lanka — a number of links tie them to one another. There is the ancestral link to the Indian sub-continent that gives common racial features to South Asians and makes them recognizable as a visible minority. Also, there are several cultural practices that South Asians continue to share, however distant their connection to the Indian sub-continent may be. Finally, there is the colonial experience that originally scattered South Asians to all parts of the world.

These historical linkages emerge as some identifiable patterns in the subject matter as well as the technique of South Asian poetry. The recurrence of these patterns in the work of South Asian poets and their relative unimportance in the work of other Canadian poets makes South Asian poetry highly interesting as a literary phenomenon both in terms of its new perspective on Canadian society and its rather unconventional relationship with the dominant literary tradition. The South Asian poet may be said to possess that double vision which comes only with alienation from the dominant group: the condition of writers as diverse as Henry James, Theodore Dreiser, Richard Wright and Salman Rushdie. This outsider is painfully aware of the contradictions that the cement of a homogeneous ideology carefully conceals from a full-fledged member of the dominant group. Consequently, South Asian poets write less about man's response to nature, the woes of age and death, the joys and pains of sexual love and other such staples of poets through the ages, and more about racism, poverty, discrimination, colonial exploitation, imperialism and ideological domination. While some South Asian poets do write on these perennial subjects, their strength as well as their preoccupations are accounted for, I believe, in terms of their otherness and visibility.[5]

The otherness of South Asian poets means that they have come to Canada, in Dabydeen's words, "mudbound in memory."[6] These poets, coming from countries which have only recently emerged from colonial domination and are plagued by poverty and political violence, continue to write about their places of origin. However, unlike other immigrant poetry, South Asian poetry does not indulge in nostalgia or what the editors of the special issue of *Canadian Ethnic Studies* termed "ethnic genealogy" (p. iii). Instead of a romanticization of the lost Eden, South Asian poetry attempts to draw the attention of the Canadian reader to the misery of poverty:

> loving you,
> I think of twisted, leprous hands,
> rains laying waste the year's harvest
> people shooting each other off
> in war
> or by accident
>
> you think I have wandered off
> into a private land of pleasure,
> leaving you lonely
> in your turbulence.
>
> but love,
> I will join you,
> my lust a trifle late perhaps,
> when I have rebuilt cities
> and caused children

to be born perfect
in a loving world,

as you lie thinking,
how long will he take.[8]

Here the South Asian poet does not remain confined by national boundaries but seems to reflect the sense of solidarity the Third World countries have come to share due to their history. Thus, Himani Bannerji from India writes poems on Victor Jara and Salvadore Allende while Asoka Weerasinghe, a Sri Lankan poet, writes about the misery of the war-torn Sahelia:

Life wrapped by naked skin
moves feebly south,
the salivatory glands parched
by dessication
and each mouth
open to gobble the hot air,
They pass neo-middens
of man, bird and mammal,
smoking under the hot sun
all scaled and bare,
where there are no flowers to bear
the lily-smell of death,
of an African "quality of life."[7]

It is apparent from the above examples that South Asian poetry abounds in images of violence, suffering and death. In a society of plenty where obesity is a national problem, a preoccupation with malnourished and diseased forms may sound distant and jarring. The South Asian poets, therefore, have to make sure that their poetry is firmly bound to the Canadian context. To ensure this, they often structure their poems to join the two realms of their experience in a meaningful way. Some of the devices they use are: letters home which talk about Canada to a person who is a stranger to Canadian ways; physical and spiritual journeys which, apart from articulating the poet's own experience as an immigrant, also bring in references to the historical journeys of the past, such as those of the *Komagata Maru* and the indentured labourers; contrasts of season — where Canadian winter often symbolizes the death of poetic inspiration as well as the lack of friendliness on the part of the host society; and dreams joining the poet's life at home with existence here as seen in his psychic life. This poem by Arnold Itwaru, for example, contrasts the two realms through the conjunctions which only dreams provide:

Half-formed, malformed, they are there in my sleep,
they are there when I awake. Explosions of
clocks and faces, of flesh and bone. I run
from them but they erupt before me. I see
them, but what are they? I've tried to forget
them, to tell myself I'm okay, you're okay,
we're all okay. I've tried to reason
them out of existence . . .

. . . behind the pages, the pictures, the
streets, children eat adults, adults eat
children, they all eat garbage, morsel to
morsel, blood for blood, spectres, caricatures,
skeletons, corpses, tumescent in endless
oceans.[9]

While the dream structure of the poem allows the poet to bring in experiences so radically alien to Canadian life, his mocking reference to the bestseller *I'm Okay, You're Okay* effectively contrasts the two worlds. With remarkable economy, the title of the bestseller underlines the poet's disappointment with the affluent west's attitude to the developing countries. The poem, while mocking the narcissism of the individualistic philosphy of the book, shows that the problems it deals with are those of affluence. Thus, in counterpointing itself against an ironic allusion, the poem gains multiplicity of meaning and resonance.

A number of South Asian poets use this strategy of ironic contrast. This they bring to bear on the poem through an allusion to a shibboleth of the dominant culture. The following poem by Bhaggiyadatta is a good example:

We came
in 747s
to sink
to the bottom
of the upheld mosaic:
to push mailcarts
("beaverbrook started this way, you know")

the natives say it's initiation
they did it to the irish
the italian the gay
but we are better
niggers

55

we take shit with
a smile
and a colour t.v.[10]

Bhaggiyadatta mocks the egalitarian pretensions of the mosaic metaphor as well as the favourite myth of North American capitalism, that of the self-made man. This satirical sparring against the powers that be stands in contrast to the thematic concerns of much recent "mainstream" Canadian poetry whose mood remains largely neo-romantic. Unlike the self-enclosed, meditative poetic mode so popular among modern Anglo-Canadian poets, the South Asian poetic mode is one of ironic relationships. The outside world is brought into the poem to provide resonances and contrasts, most of them bitterly ironic. The poems repeatedly confront and challenge social policy. Sometimes, as in Bannerji's "Terror," the note is extremely dark. This poem gives voice to the suppressed rage as well as the terror that South Asian immigrants feel under the oppression of hate messages on the telephones, broken window-panes and physical and verbal assaults. The irony in the poem is deepened by Bannerji's use of symbols derived from history and contemporary reality.

The symbolism of King George's equestrian statue in Toronto's Queen's Park arises from the fact that it was brought to Canada from India after the latter decided to discard all visual reminders of its colonial masters. For this South Asian poet, then, the statue is not merely a nice backdrop for a photograph but a painful reminder of her past and her differences with the Canadian society:

I think of my daughter, I grow afraid, I see designs against her
deep-set into their concrete structures or embossed into their
Education Act. The blue of the sky, the gold of the sun, becomes
an Aryan-eyed blonde and her spiked heels dig into my bowels.[11]

The "Aryan-eyed blonde" with "her spiked heels" becomes representative of contemporary Canadian society. The figure is based on an actual woman, a member of the Klu Klux Klan, who used to march on the Toronto streets most frequented by East Indians in the company of KKK men, taunting, threatening and terrorizing the city's visible minorities.

Judging from the tone and the subject matter of South Asian poetry, it can be said that the South Asian consciousness is out of harmony with the accepted beliefs and practices of the host society. This sense of being out of step results at times in bitter anger, as in Bannerji and Bhaggiyadatta, and at other times in playful mockery, as in Rienzi Crusz's "The Sun-Man's Poetic Five Ways":

Who, brown and strolling
down a Toronto street

came up against these black vinyl jackets
with mouths hurling their *PAKI PAKI* words like knives;
froze, then quickly thawed to his notebook:
"Color of offenders' eyes: hazel, blue, blue.
Hair: All long, like Jesus, down the nape.
Estimated educational background: T.V.'s 'Police Story,'
starring Angie Dickinson.
Home address: Paradise Blvd., Toronto
Possible motives: kicks.
So much poetry in the trajectory of crow sounds."[12]

Even though the poem shows a tremendous sense of restraint in the poet's refusal to let his hurt show, the purpose is identical to Bannerji's "Terror." The question implied is, how can a society which prides itself on its democratic institutions, allow the existence of such injustice? The perversion of the message of Jesus and the emergence of the new "heroes" referred to in the poem casually hint at the moral decay threatening this society.

Perhaps only the sufferer can tell where the shoe pinches. Thus, while "mainstream" Canadian poetry does not treat racism as an important subject, it is one of the prominent concerns of South Asian poetry. This short poem of M. Lakshmi Gill is very suggestive in its hesitant tone and its reference to the persona's colour:

> blue ice
> (O My Canada)
> can I call
> you mine
> foreign sad
> brown that I
> am[13]

Another aspect of the immigrant experience for the South Asian poet is that of being dislocated in terms of social and economic class. Even an immigrant from an affluent background might have to undergo the humiliation of becoming "lower class." As a result, immigrant writing in general is more class conscious than the rest of Canadian poetry. To cite again the editorial of *Canadian Ethnic Studies* referred to earlier, "by portraying the immigrant and ethnic experience, which has often been lived in a working-class milieu, 'ethnic' writers have provided a thematic perspective that has largely been missing at the centre of Canadian literature which, academic and élitist, has given little space to the drama of class struggle and its individual tragedies" *(p.v)*. The South Asian poet, of necessity, writes about his treatment at the hands of landlords and immigration officials, racist graffiti in public washrooms and his experiences at the workplace:

> FACE IT THERE'S AN ILLEGAL
> IMMIGRANT
> HIDING IN YOUR HOUSE
> HIDING IN YOU
> TRYING TO GET OUT!
>
> . . .
> . . .
> . . .
>
> . . .
> TRYING TO GET IN
> ON YOUR AFFLUENT FANTASIES
> AND FIFTY CENT FEARS
>
> (BUSINESSMEN CUSTOMS OFFICIALS
> DARK GLASSES INDUSTRIAL AVIATION
> POLICEMEN ILLEGAL BACHELORETTES
> SWEATSHOP KEEPERS INFORMATION CANADA
> SAYS
> "YOU CAN'T GET THEIR SMELL OFF THE WALLS"[14]

Sukhwant Hundal's "A Letter to a Friend" comments on the persona's life in Canada in the context of the mythical images of the western world's prosperity that circulate in the developing societies:

> You might have imagined me
> sitting in a chair surrounded by machines,
> touch-pushing switches with my fingers. . .
>
> How can I tell you — when pulling
> the four-by-twelve-by-twenty-two boards
> how they drag my body
> and sap its strength;
> or when holding in my hand a broom
> taller than myself
> I spick and span the floor,
> I am reminded of the good old college days
> when we used to rebuke the janitor
> for blowing dust while brooming the floor.[15]

Ironically, instead of sending this letter which lets his friend in India know "the truth," the persona writes another letter "full of colourful lies" which hides "how my self-esteem falls apart into dust. . . ."

The poem is a poignant comment on the fragility of the immigrant's psyche, battered as it is by individual and institutionalized racism. It is not only the oppressive external forces that the South Asian poet writes about, however. The poems of Uma Parameswaran give vent to another kind of fragmentation of the South Asian's sense of identity. Parameswaran writes about the conflicts present within the family itself. While this, again, is a subject common to immigrant poetry in general, the matter is further complicated for the South Asian poet by the fact that South Asian children are precluded by their skin colour from merging unobtrusively into the society at large. Written in the form of a child's monologue addressed to his mother, this poem by Parameswaran brings to light the self-hatred of a non-white child confronted by a society unwilling to respect his "differentness":

> Ma, you think you could change my name
> to Jim or David or something?
> . . .
> When the snow comes, ma,
> I'll get less brown won't I?
> It would be nice to be white,
> more like everyone else
> you know?[16]

Though the subject is extremely painful, the irony is deliberately muted. The appeal to the Canadian reader to do something about the state of affairs is made very deviously. Nonetheless, the poem is highly effective in its understatement.

Much of South Asian poetry, like this poem, bears the character of a rhetorical appeal, even when it does not address the reader directly. Ranging through various levels of irony, it insists on confronting the reader with the contradictions between the society's preaching and practice. Its achievement can be defined, in Kenneth Burke's terms, as providing us with a "perspective by incongruity." A good writer, Burke says, provides new insights by "violating the 'proprieties' of the word in its previous linkages." [17] Clearly from the examples quoted thus far, South Asian poetry is, above all, a violation of proprieties. In its constant insistence on questioning the rules of the game, as it were, it makes us aware of the ludicrousness of several solemn ceremonies. Take, for example, Dabydeen's "Señorita," which shrewdly exposes the short-comings of western aesthetic norms:

> This Señorita from the Dominican
> Republic flashes a smile;

she tells me she has attended school
in Canada, is interested in Lope de Vega
and extols the Golden Age of Spain.
I remind her of Pablo Neruda
and Nicholas Guillen,
both closer to her home.
She still smiles, professes
a dim acquaintance with the poetry
of both, talks about water imagery
In Neruda. I remind her about the latter's
fire of love, the Cuban's revolutionary
zeal. She's not impressed.
She still smiles however.


How about the poets
of the Dominican Republic?
She smiles once more. "Ah, do you
not see I have been educated
in Canada?" She protests innocently.


"Five million people there —
surely there must be poets!"
I exclaim in silent rage.
Once more the Señorita smiles —
as bewitching as a metaphor.[18]

The poem effectively points out the reasons many Third World writers feel so alienated from the western literary tradititons, even though they write in languages bequeathed to them by the colonial powers. Closer to home, it makes us aware of the structuralist-formalist stance of the literary criticism, so much in vogue in Canada, which dwells on images and symbols and other aspects of technique while disregarding the ideological and sociological aspects of literature. It also brings out the insularity of our departments of literature which rarely tread outside the European literary tradition.

Himani Bannerji's "A Savage Aesthetic," a translation of a Bengali poem by Manabendra Bandopadhyay, makes a similar point. The poem is constructed in two parts. The first half of the poem is a lecture in a poetry class while the second half is the poet's rejoinder. The poem brings out the ideological stance of an aesthetic which prides itself on its objectivity:

> *"Remember, poetry too is architecture*
> *all else is redundant except the form, the style —*
> *what you call — the texture."*
>
> . . . . .
>
> . . . and so the poetry class unending.
> Always the same. Sharp, academic
> an exhibition of smug narcissism. Full of apt
> and self-conscious quotations, allusions and message
> in a voice that plays with a joke or two,
> calculating, avoiding emotional excess.
> So stands this hour of aesthetics, an exact reflection,
> of the confidence of the glass and concrete phallus
> that arises on an erased slum or broken shanty town.[19]

Such poems reflect the disillusionment of the South Asian poets with their western literary training. For while their poetic strategies show their familiarity with it, their poems are really parodies of the dominant modes.

The South Asian poets invert western myths for ironic purposes instead of using them seriously in the way Canadian mythopoeic poets like Jay MacPherson do, for instance. In "Lady Icarus," Dabydeen applies the myth to the story of Maria, an aspiring immigrant from Equador who fell to her death when trying to escape from detention by immigration authorities.[20] Suniti Namjoshi's "Philomel" points out an aspect of the myth thus far unexplored:

> She had her tongue ripped out, and then she sang
> down through the centuries. So that it seems only
> fitting that the art she practices should be art for
> art's sake, and never spelt out, no — never reduced
> to its mere message — that would appal.
>
> (Tereus raped Philomela and cut out her tongue in
> order to silence her. She was then transformed into
> the "poetic" nightingale which sings so sweetly through
> western tradition.)[21]

The inversion of western myths, the ironic use of forms, the retorts to western writers and critics, all point out the South Asian poets' sense of the unsuitability of the western literary tradition for their purposes. Itwaru, for example, clears out his territory by removing the familiar landmarks that the western reader takes for granted:

NOTICE
ENTER THIS WILDERNESS AT YOUR OWN RISK. THERE
ARE NO VIRGILS HERE, BEATRICE AWAITS NOWHERE.
THERE ARE CANOEISTS, BUT YOU WILL FIND NO CHARON.
YOU SHOULD BE WARNED THAT THE RIVERS ARE POISON
OUS. OTHER THAN YOU THERE ARE NO DANGEROUS ANI-
MALS. [22]

Itwaru, like so many modern Third World poets, finds the idiom of western poetry inappropriate for him. The long tradition the western poet relies on in creating his meaning is discarded as so much jetsam. This has to be done because the tradition does not represent the history of a Third World poet like Itwaru. Of course, the poet discards it only symbolically. The things to be rejected have to be named if others are to understand this act of rebellion. Conventions have to be used if only in order to be stood on their head.

These constant inversions show how difficult the task of the South Asian poet actually is when compared to that of a writer who feels at home in his tradition. Salman Rushdie has described it in his novel *Shame* while expressing his frustration about rendering concepts of a culture in a foreign tongue which has no equivalents for them:

> This word: shame. No, I must write it in its original form, not in this peculiar language tainted by wrong concepts and the accumulated detritus of its owners' unrepented past, this Angrezi in which I am forced to write, and so for ever alter what is written. ... Sharam, that's the word. For which this paltry 'shame' is a wholly inadequate translation. ... A short word, but one containing encyclopaedias of nuance. [23]

Raja Rao, the celebrated Indian novelist, made the same point in 1937 while describing his efforts to tell a story from "the contemporary annals" of his village: "The telling has not been easy. One has to convey in a language that is not one's own the spirit that is one's own." [24] The titles of the works of South Asian poets indicate the nature of the difficulties they face in communicating their vision here in Canada; titles like *A Separate Sky, Distances, Shattered Songs* and *Rupture* declare their sense of working against the current.

When the South Asian poet inverts accepted meanings, he is at least using a familiar idiom, though in a different key. However, as one cannot remain in a state of perpetual reaction, the South Asian poet invents his own language. The difficulties of this task are well outlined in Dabydeen's "For the Sun Man," a poem addressed to a fellow South Asian poet, Rienzi Crusz. The poet commends Crusz for his ability" to pluck parables / from the Buddha's core" while he himself, "being so much / like the west," is suffering from a loss of creativity. The poem states the need for creating new metaphors as the old ones no longer work. [25] The "Sun Man" of the poem's title is Crusz's mythic persona and occurs in several of his poems. The persona allows Crusz to amalgamate the two segments of his life in a meaningful way while at the same time it works as a readily available device with which to build further.

A number of poets "pluck parables" from their South Asian past. Surjeet Kalsey's "Siddhartha Does Penance Again"[26] compares the journey of a modern-day immigrant to that of the Buddha leaving home in his search for enlightenment. The poem plays with the difference between the two Siddharthas and the nature of their journeys. Suniti Namjoshi's *Feminist Fables* borrows its form from the ancient Indian tales of the *Panchatantra*. Using the tales from the *Panchatantara* as well as nursery rhymes, classical mythology and *The Arabian Nights*, Namjoshi comments satirically on the place of women in modern society. It is a highly original work which is complex without becoming inaccessible.

Perhaps, for an uninitiated reader who has had no cross-cultural experience, the use of such resources will be difficult to comprehend. However, the South Asian poet is compelled to use them, as nothing else can be substituted in their place. Uma Parameswaran's "Ganga Jal" demonstrates the importance of myth and ritual for poetry as well as the fact that language is not merely grammar and syntax but buried culture. For "Ganga Jal" is a phrase that stirs some very profound emotions in a Hindu mind. It means the water of the holy river Ganga which is needed in Hindu homes to perform several sacraments related to birth, initiation and death. Ganga water is poured into the mouth of the dying person and after cremation ashes of Hindus are strewn in the river. Every believing Hindu, hence, keeps at least a bottle of Ganga water at home. Given this context, the reader realizes by the end of the first stanza that the poem is about imminent death:

> I heard him come in the door
> and straight to the kitchen.
> He had snowflakes in his hair
> And his face was white as any neighbour's
> All blood from it in his burning eyes
> His boots formed an instant puddle
> as he stood at the kitchen door.
> Gangajal, he said, I need Ganga-jal.[27]

The poem captures a very intimate aspect of South Asian life in Canada. The household gods, the container of Gangajal, the rituals of birth and death: who

63

else will write about these aspects of South Asian experience except a South Asian poet? The poem is extremely moving as it dramatically renders the anguish of dying so far away from home and traditions. However, alien as its allusions are to Canadian readers, it is doubtful if it would have the same impact on a person unacquainted with the Indian ethos.

No doubt, a poetry that contains unfamiliar names of poets, gods, historical figures, Third World personalities, inversions of conventional poetic idiom and, at times, rhythms and diction unfamiliar to the North American ear can seem obscure. However, if literature were taught in a multicultural context, as a means of promoting an understanding of the dependency of literature on culture, tradition and history, South Asian poetry in Canada could serve as a useful means of comparison. It could then provide a valuable tool for teachers of literature in introducing their students to ways of apprehending the world which are different from the one they have been brought up with. Ioan Davies' remarks about the poetry of Bannerji and Itwaru can be applied to the contribution of the South Asian poets in general: "Their uniqueness is that they are representatives of a generation of writers in Canada who are not part of the mainstream of our literature." Their works, Davies goes on to say, are "the expressions of an otherness against a hegemony in which the terms of reference are dictated by the preoccupations of those who have established themselves as the centre-pieces of a dominating culture."[28] That act in itself, of making the dominating culture self-conscious, is a contribution which should allot South Asian poetry, along with the literature of other racial and ethnic minorities in Canada, an important niche in Canadian literature.

# NOTES

[1] Robert Kroetsch, Tamara J. Palmer and Beverly J. Rasporich, "Introduction: Ethnicity and Canadian Literature." *Canadian Ethnic Studies,* 14: 1 (1982), iv.

[2] The phrase "South Asian" is applied to denote immigrants who have come to Canada either directly from the Indian sub-continent, i.e. India, Pakistan, Bangladesh and Sri Lanka, or have ancestral links with the sub-continent. Thus, many Caribbean immigrants to Canada are descendants of indentured labourers from northern India who were lured there by the British in the nineteenth century.

[3] See Bharati Mukherjee, "An Invisible Woman," *Saturday Night,* March 1981, pp. 36-40.

[4] See the following selected bibliography.

[5] Insofar as Michael Ondaatje's work does not speak of his otherness and visibility, he is excluded from this essay. In the previous essay I have already commented on these omissions in his work. Since this paper is concerned with identifying the similarities and preoccupations of South Asian poets in general, it would be inappropriate to devote time to criticising Ondaatje's work, especially since that would also mean taking issue with several prominent Canadian critics who have been effusive in their praise of Ondaatje. Here I would only like to say that I have been troubled by a lack of awareness on the part of Canadian critics as to Ondaatje's disregard for his past as well as the local reality. I draw their attention to this comment from a fellow Sri Lankan which seems to fit Ondaatje very well:

> Glimpsing the headlines in the papers,
> tourists scuttle for cover, cancel their options
> on rooms with views of temple and holy mountain.
> "Flash-point in Paradise." "The racial pot boils over."
> And even the gone away boy
> who had hoped to find lost roots, lost loves,
> lost talent even, out among the palms,
> makes timely return giving thanks
> that Toronto is quite romantic enough
> for his purposes.

Yasmine Gooneratne, "Big Match," *Toronto South Asian Review,* 2: 2 (1983), 1

[6] Cyril Dabydeen, "New Life,"*This Planet Earth* (Ottawa: Borealis Press1979), p. 64.

[7] S. Padmanab, "Night-Song," *Songs of the Slave* (Cornwall, Ont.: Vesta Publications, 1977), p. 26.

[8] Asoka Weerasinghe, "Sahelia" in *Poems for Jeannie* (Cornwall, Ont.: Vesta Publications, 1976), p. 27.

[9] Arnold Itwaru, "Shattered Songs," *Nebula,* First Quarter (1981), 55.

[10] Krisantha Sri Bhaggiyadatta, "My Family," in *Domestic Bliss* (Toronto: Domestic Bliss, 1981), pp. 9-10.

[11] Himani Bannerji, "Terror," in *A Separate Sky* (Toronto: Domestic Bliss. 1982), p. 25.

[12] Rienzi Crusz, "The Sun-Man's Poetic Five Ways," *Toronto South Asian Review,* 1: 1 (1982), 54.

[13] M. Lakshmi Gill, "Song," in *First clearing (an immigrant's tour of life) poems* (Manila, Philippines: Estaniel Press, 1972), p. 6.

[14] Bhaggiyadatta, *Domestic Bliss,* p. 23.

[15] Sukhwant Hundal, "A Letter to a Friend," transl. Surjeet Kalsey, *Toronto South Asian Review,* 2: 1 (1983), 77, 78.

[16] Uma Parameswaran, untitled poem, *Toronto South Asian Review,* 1: 3 (1982), 15.

[17] Kenneth Burke, *Permanence and Change: An Anatomy of Change,* rev. ed. (New York: Bobbs-Merril, 1935), p. 90.

[18] Cyril Dabydeen, *Goatsong* (Ottawa: Mosaic Press, 1977), p. 28.

[19] Bannerji, "A Savage Aesthetic," translated from Bengali by the poet, in *A Separate Sky,* pp. 46-47.

[20] Dabydeen, "Lady Icarus," in *Goatsong,* p. 16.

[21] Suniti Namjoshi, "Philomel," in *Feminist Fables* (London: Sheba Feminist Publishers) p. 102.

[22] Itwaru, p. 54.

[23] Salman Rushdie, *Shame* (Calcutta: Rupa, 1983), pp. 38-39.

[24] Raja Rao, Foreword to *Kanthapura,* 2nd ed. (Madras, India: Oxford U P 1974), p.v.

[25] Cyril Dabydeen, "For the Sun Man," in *Elephants Make Good Stepladders* (London, Ont.: Third Eye, 1982), p. 51.

[26] Surjeet Kalsey, "Siddhartha Does Penance Again," *Toronto South Asian Review,* 2: 1 (1983), 75-76.

[27] Uma Parameswaran, "Gangajal," unpublished poem.

[28] Ioan Davies, "Senses of Place," *Canadian Forum,* April 1983, p. 34.

# A Selected Bibliography of South Asian Poetry in Canada

Bannerji, Himani. *A Separate Sky*. Toronto: Domestic Bliss, 1982.

Bhaggiyadatta. Krisantha Sri. *Domestic Bliss*. Toronto: Domestic Bliss, 1981.

Crusz, Rienzi. *Flesh and Thorn*. Stratford, Ont.: The Pasdeloup Press, 1974.

————. *Elephant and Ice*. Erin, Ont.: The Porcupine's Quill, 1980.

Dabydeen, Cyril. *Poems in Recession*. Georgetown, Guyana: Sadeek Press, 1972.

————. *Distances*. Fredericton, N.B.: Fiddlehead Poetry Books, 1977.

————. *Goatsong*. Ottawa: Mosaic Press, 1977.

————. *This Planet Earth*. Ottawa: Borealis Press, 1979.

————. *Elephants Make Good Stepladders. London, Ont*: Third Eye, 1982.
Gill, M. Lakshmi. *During Rain, I Plant Chrysanthemums*. Toronto: The Ryerson Press, 1966.

————. *Mind-Walls: Poems*. Fredericton N.B.: Fiddlehead Poetry Books, 1970.

————. *First clearing (an immigrant's tour of life) poems*. Manila, Philippines: Estaniel Press, 1972.

————. *Novena to St. Jude Thaddeus: Poems*. Fredericton: N.B.: Fiddlehead Poetry Books, 1979.

Gool, Réshard. *In Medusa's Eye*. 1972; rpt. ed. Charlottetown: Square Deal Publications.

Itwaru, Arnold. *Shattered Songs*. Toronto. Aya Press, 1982.

Kalsey, Surjeet. *Speaking to the Winds,* London, Ont.: The Third Eye Publications. 1982. Translation of author's Punjabi work.

Namjoshi, Suniti. *Cyclone in Pakistan*. Calcutta, India: Writer's Workshop, 1971.

————. *The Jackass and the Lady*. Calcutta, India: Writer's Workshop, 1980.

————. *Feminist Fables*. London: Sheba Feminist Publishers, 1981.

————. *The Authentic Lie*. Fredericton, N.B.: Fiddlehead Poetry Books, 1982.

Ondaatje, Michael. *The Dainty Monsters*. Toronto: Coach House Press, 1967.

————. *the man with seven toes*. Toronto: Coach House Press, 1969.

————. *The Collected Works of Billy the Kid: Left Handed Poems*. Toronto: Anansi, 1970.

————. *Rat Jelly*. Toronto: Coach House Press, 1973.

————. *There's a Trick with a Knife I Am Learning to do: Poems 1963 to 1978*. Toronto: McClelland and Stewart, 1979.

————. *Running in the Family*. Toronto: McClelland and Stewart, 1982.

Padmanab, S. *Songs of the Slave*. Cornwall, Ont.: Vesta Publications, 1977.

Parameswaran, Uma. *Cyclic Hope Cyclic Pain*. Calcutta, India: Writer's Workshop, 1974.

————."Trishanku." In progress.

Weerasinghe, Asoka. *Spring Quartet*. U.K.: Breakthru Press, 1972.

————. *Poems for Jeannie*. Cornwall, Ont.: Vesta Publications, 1976.

————. *Poems in November*. Ottawa: Commoner's Publishing, 1977.

————. *Hot Tea and Cinnamon Buns*. Cornwall, Ont.: Vesta Publications, 1980.

————. *Home Again Lanka*. Ottawa: Commoner's, 1981.

————. *Selected Poems*. 1958-1983. Cornwall, Ont.: Vesta Publications, 1983.

# The Sri Lankan Poets in Canada:
## An Alternative View

One of the most interesting cultural phenomena of the last few years is the emergence in Canada of the visible minority writer against the background of a predominantly "Anglo-Gaelic" literary scene. A large number of the so-called hyphenated Canadians are giving voice to the experiences of Canada's racial and ethnic minorties. These writers, coming from varied cultural and literary traditions, are not only challenging the erstwhile "official" cultural image of Canada, but, in the process of doing so, they are also introducing ways of apprehending that go beyond the Anglo-American tradition of literature that has dominated Canadian writing. Not all visible minority writers, of course, manage to be original and authentic. Many of them are lost to their communities when they find acceptance amidst the "official" bastions of culture. They, then, try to imitate the accepted ways of writing that will keep them in grants and on the poetry-reading circuit.

As someone deeply interested in the ideology of culture, I find it very fascinating to observe Canadian writers of visible minority backgrounds in terms of the processes of cultural domination. Their works, and their relative acceptance or rejection by the mainstream, are good object lessons in the politics of literary production. In their role of the "other," they compel us to take stock of Canadian literature from a vantage point that the mainstream Canadian critics rarely employ in their preoccupation with nuances of technique and their total disregard for such issues as history, politics, race, and class.

A study of the works of the poets of Sri Lankan origin presently writing in Canada will bear out the truth of the remarks I have made. For, while as Sri Lankans they are being seen here as a group, a more motley group would be hard to conceive of. For example, Michael Ondaatje is a name that would be hard to miss for a student of Canadian literature. But it is doubtful that this same student has heard of Rienzi Crusz, Krisantha Sri Bhaggiyadatta or Asoka Weerasinghe. These other Sri Lankan poets should also be of interest to the critic when analysing Ondaatje's work, for comparison and contrast. This has not happened, since the mainstream Canadian critics as a rule disregard the categories I have mentioned above. Under the star system that operates in the area of Canadian criticism, Michael Ondaatje has won accolades for work of questionable merit while other Sri Lankan poets have not even received a mention.

In this paper, then, I have attempted to set a balance. I wish to assess Ondaatje's work in order to bring out certain disturbing questions that assail me when reading him as well as to comment, in some detail, on the work of his compatriots. As the questions I am going to raise have to do with some basic assumptions prevalent in the western world about literature and its role as a social institution, my paper is also a critique of the predominant modes of criticism in Canada.

Ondaatje's work has failed to appeal to me. However, as a writer who has won several prestigious awards and whose work has inspired extravagant praise from established Canadian critics, his work continued to challenge me to pinpoint the reasons for my lack of appreciation. The result of that struggle was my paper, "Two Responses to Otherness: The Poetry of Michael Ondaatje and Cyril Dabydeen." Though the paper was read at the Learneds Conference at Vancouver in 1983 and subsequently published in 1985, several more papers have been published on Ondaatje since then, reiterating the accepted view. Some colleagues of mine have taken my paper as a kind of joke and have taken to teasing me off and on about my stand on Ondaatje. I suppose joke is the only response left in the absence of a rational answer. Typically, when I asked one of them to describe what was so good about Ondaatje's work, all he could say was that this poet's line was so "cool"!

Such impressionistic appreciation does not really constitute an assessment of a writer's work. This, however, is the mode in which most critical commentaries on Ondaatje are written. Nothing is explained. Excellence is taken for granted rather than proved. As Sam Solecki is one of the important names in the Canadian literary establishment, and as he has written several papers on Ondaatje, let me quote a somewhat long excerpt from his latest piece on Ondaatje in order to give the reader a flavour of this kind of literary criticism:

> He's among the handful of contemporary poets whom you can sense in almost any line of their work. In Canada, only Atwood has as strong a signature — an impress breathing in and through a line — colouring the work and establishing, constituting Camus' 'climate.' The climate of a world created book by book, never the same season, yet from *The Dainty Monsters* to *Running in the Family* always the same world.
>
> What changes is the creation of the illusion that his 'exclusive' world is becoming less 'exclusive,' that the later work will 'shave' the beard in the photo (*Coming Through Slaughter*, p. 133) and reveal a true 'self-portrait.' The illusion depends on one of the tricks he's learned to do; he uses valorized words like mother, father, sister, brother to distract the reader from noticing that for him, as for the best poets, 'I' is a third-person pronoun, a word whose referents lie in the poem creating it for the occasion. Even *Billy the Kid* and *Coming Through Slaughter* tease the reader with the image of self as other, other as self.[1]

What I have gleaned from Solecki and other critics is that Ondaatje's poetry is concerned with the act of creation itself. The chief figure in his work is the artist who is seen "as gunman, as spider, as taxidermist, as Audubon, as cage-maker, as necrophiliac, as insurance executive, as collector, as editor, as suicide." [2] The artist, according to this point of view, is caught up in an endless dualism. He tries to capture "reality" and in that attempt "murders" it. The artistic process, then, is a series of disappointments and the artist constantly faces the danger of going mad. He lives on the "edge," doing a dangerous balancing act.

The trouble I have with this subject matter is that it is too limited to be made the basis of an entire *oeuvre*. Secondly, it is a rather romantic version of the artist who is always struggling against the onslaught of madness brought about by an "intolerable creative situation." [3] The artist in this version is not a participant in the social process, he does not get drawn into the act of living, which involves the need to deal with the burning issues of his time, such as poverty, injustice, exploitation, racism, sexism, etc., and he does not write about other human beings unless they happen to be artists — or members of his own family.

Ondaatje, the artist, makes poems out of other artists such as Victor Coleman, Wallace Stevens and Henri Rousseau. He writes about other artists who have become insane such as Buddy Bolden. He writes about historical figures such as Billy the Kid and Mrs. Fraser, twisting them into exemplifications of his pet theory. It is amazing to see how one can endlessly write about the act of writing: what is known in fashionable circles as deconstruction. The poem is supposedly made and unmade in front of one's eyes. And it does not need the real world at all. Its subject is itself.

Coming from a cultural milieu in which literature is expected to say something about the world, I must admit that this kind of poetry fails to touch me in any significant way. While one or two poems on the act of writing are acceptable to me, to come across this as the "theme" in work after work is simply boring.

However, if inanity was the only problem with Ondaatje's work, it would not be so bad. What is particularly objectionable is his misuse of historical figures: figures whose lives have acquired a certain range of meanings and associations are appropriated by Ondaatje for a rather nonserious purpose.

*The Man with Seven Toes,* [4] for example, deals with the Australian legend of Mrs. Fraser, a nineteenth century white woman who was shipwrecked and spent some time with the aborigines in the bush before finding her way to the white settlement with the help of a runaway convict. Australian artists such as the painter Sidney Nolan and the novelist Patrick White have used the legend to comment on the injustice done towards the convicts and the aborigines by the Australian ruling class. However, in Ondaatje's version, such issues have been totally eliminated. Mrs. Fraser is another one of those characters who have travelled to the "edge." The aborigines and the convicts are portrayed as rapists as well as uninhibited noble savages. The rapes, however, serve a positive role in the education of Mrs. Fraser, according to Ondaatje and his critics. While colonization, which resulted in the oppression of the convicts and the extermination of the aborigines, has no place in Ondaatje's version, the poem tells us, in the words of Sam Solecki (if I use him so often, it is because he has written a total of five papers on Ondaatje, besides several sporadic comments and reviews), that civilization is very tenuous and chaos hides right under the veneer. Needless to say, such statements are presented as self-evident truths about human nature and civilization.

*Coming Through Slaughter* [5] purports to be about the life of Buddy Bolden, one of the pioneers of jazz. However, Bolden is interesting to Ondaatje only because he went mad and spent the last thirty years of his life in a mental asylum. According to Ondaatje, Bolden went mad because he never repeated himself, always trying to create his notes afresh. "Bolden's music was spontaneous, raw, impermanent."[6] Bolden, like the other characters of Ondaatje, lived on the "edge" because of the demands of his art. "He skillfully balanced order and chaos, creation and destruction."[7] In this Bolden Ondaatje sees his own struggles with insanity and records them in a passage which is quoted by almost every critic writing on *Coming Through Slaughter*.

While detailed studies have been made of the imagery, texture, symbolism, allusions and what not in this work, no critic has asked whether Bolden went mad for the reason Ondaatje has given. Now I do not believe that writers have to give the literal truth. But as someone I met at Vancouver commented after hearing my paper on Ondaatje, Bolden's skin colour is entirely ignored in the book. *Coming Through Slaughter* makes nothing of the fact that Bolden was born only twelve years after the Civil War, or of the fact that jazz at this time had no appeal to the whites and that Bolden's audiences were entirely black. There is nothing in the book as to the fact that Bolden, though he was "King Bolden" to his black fans, did not exist for the newspapers or the custodians of the official culture. We do not learn from *Coming Through Slaughter* that Bolden wrote lyrics such as this:

> I thought I heer'd Abe Lincoln shout,
> Rebels close down them plantations and let all
> them niggers out.
> I'm positively sure I heer'd Mr. Lincoln shout.
> I thought I heard Mr. Lincoln say,
> Rebels close them plantations and let all them
> niggers out.

You gonna lose this war, git on your knees and pray,
That's the words I heer'd Mr. Lincoln say.[8]

One would not come across the fact in *Coming Through Slaughter* that Bolden's mother had been a slave. The Buddy Bolden of Ondaatje has no colour. His problems are entirely related to his art. It does not matter that he had become fatherless by seven and was raised by a mother who worked as a domestic for white families. (If one wants to know about the impact of such things on black artists such as Bolden, one would have to read Billie Holiday's autobiography, *Lady Sings the Blues*.)

Ondaatje has misrepresented black history and black experience in the service of a very dubious cause. He has ignored three centuries of racism and oppression suffered by the black people in America. The distortions of *Coming Through Slaughter* become apparent when it is compared with books by and about black musicians and seen in the context of the heavy odds they struggled against. All this has been ignored not only by Ondaatje but also by his critics.

Similar and equally dangerous distortions are present in *Billy the Kid*[9] Ondaatje does not explore the causes of Billy's violence. He does not go into the nature of his relationship with the Chisum family. He does not explore the Western as an integral part of American culture. All we get here are close-ups of slaughtered people. History, legend, culture, ideology are matters beyond Ondaatje's ken. And their misrepresentation has not been remarked upon.

In *Running in the Famly,* [10] the subject is Ondaatje's family, set against the backdrop of his native Sri Lanka (which he refers to as Ceylon). In an earlier essay, I have criticized the book and its reviewers for "exoticising." I was quite pleased to come across a review by a Sri Lankan critic who had similar reactions. Writing in *Kaduwa*, Qadri Ismail, the editor of this University of Ceylon journal, has this to say about the book:

> Orientalism, to simplify Edward Said's thesis, is the tendency western scholars have, when writing on the east and are unable to comprehend it fully, to go after the exotic element — in the process painting a most inauthentic picture of what really happens. This is not limited to western writers however; eastern writers, for many reasons — commercial and cultural, make the same lapses. Michael Ondaatje is most certainly guilty of this in his latest publication.
>
> This is the way most of the book is written. ... People sent back from Oxford for setting fire to their room; men and women indulging — and how! — in fantastic drunken escapades; thalagoya eating and snakes running amok in the house; a mad and very drunk Major in the Ceylon Light Infantry running riot — and stark naked — in the Kadugannawa tunnel; the same man, drunk again, throttling five mongrel dogs; another woman, also drunk, breaking the necks of dozens of chickens.

...They led most eventful lives but Ondaatje doesn't bother to extract any meaning from it all. (Maybe it had none, but it is the author's responsibility to point this out.)... He calls Lakadasa Wikkramasinha a "powerful and angry poet"; in contrast, Ondaatje's poems which litter the book, are beautifully written — and insipid. He tells us nothing of the colonial experience — or of himself.[11]

Ismail's perceptive criticism brings out an aspect western critics continue to ignore: would it not be worthwhile for them to find out what Sri Lankans might have to say about Ondaatje's work? For it, and critical responses to it, raise problems that writers and critics in the Third World have become acutely conscious of — the western patronage of "exotic" writers and the resulting distortions in the local culture, the impact of western forms in the colonial era and the Third World writers' need to break out of them, and, finally, the need to forge new critical yardsticks which confront the issues of colonialism and neocolonialism.

In her "Cultural Interaction in Modern Sri Lankan Poetry Written in English," Yasmine Gooneratne points to the pernicious effects of colonialism on the native culture. As in other colonised countries, "the Sri Lankan reader of English was encouraged to ignore and ultimately to forget, the literary traditions of monastery, court and village that had accumulated over centuries among singers and writers of Sinhala and Tamil."[12] As a result, the "English verse of early twentieth century Sri Lanka is not only derivative and imitative of a whole range of European writers, but limited in its themes; and these limitations stem from a crippling concept of genuine poetry as being the product of other cultures rather than of one's own, as well as from a severely restricted view of the function of literature as a whole."[13]

Gooneratne shows that Sri Lankan poets continue to face the problems of derivativeness and colonial relationship with the metropolis. Ironically, Canadian literary values are such that these aspects are never taken into consideration.

When one turns to the other poets of Sri Lankan origin, one comes across a spectrum of attitudes and poetic strategies. One sees different levels of success in manipulating western poetic forms to give expression to the identity of being a Sri Lankan and a visible minority in Canada. For these are themes untouched in the Anglo-American mainstream and the poet who wants to give voice to them must go elsewhere for tutelage.

Rienzi Crusz's work interests me because of the struggle that I perceive going on between his different voices. Some of his work *is* exotic and paints colourful portraits of Sri Lanka deeply swathed in nostalgia. For example:

When winter comes,
he crawls
into his sun-dial nerves

74

and sleeps
with myths and shibboleths,
as central heating steals
under his dark eye-lids,
to dream of blue Ceylon,
where palms bend
their coconut breasts
to the morning sun,
and Nuwera-Eliya's valley
oozes with the fragrance of tea,
the sun-stroked fishermen swearing
under their salty breath
as they clown
with the rush of toddy
in their black skulls.[14]

The passage points out Crusz's weaknesses as well as strengths. While he has a good grasp of rhythm and word music, and knows how to evoke pleasing images, the passage is no more than a word picture. The winter-summer contrast is a bit too obvious and one gets tired of the sun-man formula. Then, like Ondaatje, Crusz seems to like writing poems about making poems, though not to the same extent. "Poem in the Light of Total Darkness" is a good example:

Null and void are my drooping eyes,
flamboyant hair, my gravel voice.
Only the poem speaks
with the sea's haunting boom,
the delicate twitter of paddy-birds.
Soon, the taste of honey and curd
will grow in your mouth.[15]

"Poem in Peacock Blue," similarly, is about the poet musing on whether he will write his poem in peacock blue or red or yellow or aquamarine, etc.:

Aquamarine, Tahitian,
Robin's Egg, Delphinium Blue:
sea-colours cannot be trusted,
they flirt too much, too fast
with the moving sun,
the magic fingers of the wind.[16]

Poems like this are cloyingly rich in their imagery and euphony and short on meaning. I wish Crusz had more engaging themes to better utilize his technical virtuosity. For when Crusz does have an interesting theme, the results are extremely satisfying. At his best, Crusz blends his Sri Lankan and Canadian experiences to make profound comments on both societies. "Conversations with God About My Present Whereabouts" is an excellent poem, rich both technically and thematically:

> True, I often miss
>  the sensuous touch of fingers
> on the shying touch-me-not,
> the undergrowth's pink badge of bruise,
> cacophony of crows,
> the rain that pelted my thin bones.
>
> But I am perfect now.
> Seduced on shaven grass,
> my barbecue glows
> like a small hell,
> the pork-chops kindle,
> the Molson cool,
> I wear the turban of urban pride.[17]

The poem half-humorously compares Sri Lanka and Canada as two ways of living. Crusz brings out the ambiguities of an immigrant's experience with great skill. The poem subtly criticizes the packaged, programmed life in a postindustrial society and implies that life in Sri Lanka, however hard in terms of material comforts, was more authentic.

"The Maker" is another poem which represents Crusz at his best. Multivalent in its ambiguities, it examines the meaning of colonial experience. It seems to ask: did the maker create the black man of the colonized countries so that the white man could come and destroy him? In so doing, the poem makes fun of concepts such as "manifest destiny" and "the white man's burden."

Crusz's work, despite its uneven quality, retains one's interest because of the authenticity of his struggle to forge a voice that will be able to tell the world about a black man's life:

> Dark I am,
> and darkly do I sing
> with mucus
> in my throat.[18]

Asoka Weerasinghe is another poet from Sri Lanka who faces problems similar to Crusz's. Like Robert Burns, these two poets succeed most when they write about what is close to the bone. Close to the bone, untramelled by fetters of convention and propriety. However, while every poem of Crusz is polished and technically satisfying, Weerasinghe seems to write too much and revise too little. Many poems which begin very promisingly lose momentum by the final stanza, which comes across as an anticlimax spoiling the whole effect. Sometimes the choice of a single wrong word destroys an otherwise worthwhile poem. One also comes across ungrammatical and syntactically awkward expressions which could have been easily corrected. But for these problems Weerasinghe could be a better poet. For he does write on a wide range of themes and manages to attain moments of beauty. One wishes he could sustain them longer.

"The Birth of Insurgents" is a good example of Weerasinghe's weaknesses:

> I was at home
> when April showered
> guns and bullets.
> Eight borrowed helicopters
> droned like ailing mosquitoes,
> while offspring of the guilty
> book-paddled in Paris and Oxford.[19]

The poem is ruined for me by "ailing mosquitoes." Its poignancy turns to bathos when one is forced to think how to distinguish an ailing mosquito from a healthy one.

However, Weerasinghe, despite his shortcomings, has managed to write several good poems. His political poems are especially interesting. Poems such as "The Birth of Insurgents," "Looking Back," "Sahelia," "Drought" and "Mary March" read beautifully. "Dev, (the child minstrel)," is quite representative of Weerasinghe at his best:

> An injured ivory-toothed serphina
> half his size,
> loaded on one side,
> strapped across the clavicle
> breathe into a voice
> the scrubbing hunger pains
> of a shrunken stomach.
> The frail tawny arm
> raised in humble salute,
> he will sing en route
> under a coconut palm

to a camel on burning sands,
for sweat-stained paisa
thrown from foreign hands.[20]

The poem appeals through its quiet simplicity which, nonetheless, is rife with ironies. Dev, the child, cannot assuage his hunger despite working hard at an early age, while tourists come searching for paradise in a country which cannot even provide for its children. Poems such as "Dev" continue to attract me to Weerasinghe's poetry despite his lapses.

Krisantha Sri Bhaggiyadatta is a poet who has emerged relatively recently. His first collection, *Domestic Bliss,* [21] was published in 1981. Unlike Weerasinghe and Crusz, Bhaggiyadatta came to Canada when he was young (sixteen). His is a young and angry voice. Racism has been the most important experience in his life in Canada, forcing him to think about his identity as a black person from a country with a colonial past.

This thinking comes out in his poetry as biting satires on racism that all the rhetoric of multiculturalism fails to hide, on multinational corporations in their role as exploiters of the Third World, on the pious pronouncements of politicians that belie the practice of their governments, on the western media that distort reality, and, finally, on those in his own community whom he sees as bootlickers of the establishment. Bhaggiyadatta's barbs and bitter ironic thrusts remind me of the poetry of the Augustans who attacked their rulers with great and savage gusto.

In poem after poem, Bhaggiyadatta manages to hold the reader with his gift for satire. His inventiveness is quite amazing. "What City? Ethnicity? How to Make an Ethnic Newspaper," for example, is over a hundred lines long and striking for the richness of its arsenal. Shaft after shaft comes raining down, each more powerful than the other. One recognizes in the poem a certain truth about politics in Ontario. In the effective portrayal of that truth lies Bhaggiyadatta's strength. The poem purports to offer a recipe for keeping an ethnic newspaper afloat:

> Place as many photographs of the Prime Minister,
> Minister of Immigration, Secretary of State for
> Multiculturalism, Minister of Citizenship and (then)
> Culture, Leaders of the Parliamentary Opposition
> Federal Provincial Regional Municipal
> on the front pages . . .

Praise the Public Realtions Department
(from whom all advertising contracts flow)
Do not question terms of tender, supply and
service, lease and licensing, hiring and firing
Diversify instead

in group homes, nursing homes,
homes for the aged, blue and white movies,
hair sprays, hair designers, hair straighteners,
cosmeticians, jewellers, wholesale meat specialists
weight loss clinics, spices, beauty salons . . .

Accept advertisements from the government
to tell Pape & Danforth, Lansdowne & College,
Bathurst & Bloor, Jane & Finch:
"Together We Are Ontario"
while they tell
Sarnia, London, Owen Sound, Peterborough, North Bay, Ottawa
"Immigrants are taking away our jobs"[22]

Bhaggiyadatta's poetry is markedly different not only from that of the other
Sri Lankan poets who continue to use the western lyrical-meditative mode, but
also from the kind of poetry so prolifically being written in Canada: personal,
slightly anguished, mournful about the past, laden with memories of childhood.
As Charles Altieri commented in his *Enlarging the Temple: New Directions in
American Poetry During the 1960s,* this lyrical-meditative poetry has nar-
rowed down the range of poetic voices and divorced poetry from any active
participation in the public life.[23] I agree with Altieri that modern poetry has been
reduced to renderings of love, nature, metaphysics and imagination.

Of course, when one has a cause, or one feels deeply, one is angry. Feminists
like Adrienne Rich have managed to break out of the mould. The black poets
of America have broken away from the established forms to give voice to their
history and their struggle. In Canada, minority poets like Bhaggiyadatta,
Dionne Brand, Himani Bannerji and Cyril Dabydeen are engaged in something
similar. When one reads their works, one comes across names from Africa,
Asia and Latin America.

I specifially asked Bhaggiyadatta how he has made this journey when the
dominant mode of poetry here is so restrictive. He says he has been  vastly
influenced by black American poets who taught him to "curse." He says he is
bored by the major names in western poetry who have nothing to say about his
life in the here and now, or how it came to be that way.

I find it very interesting to observe how a poet chooses his strategies.

Bhaggiyadatta, for example, refuses to write what he calls "trees" poems. He says that though he is as affected by the beauty of nature as any other human being, he cannot separate it from his other experiences. Moreover, he fears that it is the "trees" poems which the anthologists and commentators will pick while turning a deaf ear to his political poetry. Bhaggiyadatta is a very promising and a very unusual poet. Though he may never crack the big league, he takes poetry to people who have rarely been spoken to by the modern western poets. He recites his poetry at Toronto's Trojan Horse café, union meetings, picket lines, the popular Kensington Market and informal gatherings. Poetry, he says, is one of his weapons in his fight for justice and dignity. Here is another example of his craft:

> in the middle of the disappearances
> in Argentina
> when Canada was executing
> a deal with it
> on nuclear power,
> the head of the
> Atomic Energy Commission said:
> the business of business
> is business[24]

There are some other names that deserve mention. Tyrrell Mendis published his collection, *Broken Petals,* [25] in 1965 and continues to write sporadically. He is, however, a rather limited poet. His subject, according to the dust jacket of *Broken Petals,* is "love," "pain," "grief" and "frustration." He writes about what is known in the liberal parlance as "the human condition." This human condition, unfortunately, is too abstract and too melancholic. Mendis' new poems don't seem to be much different from his early work. He is a good case study in what literature curricula in India and Sri Lanka, heavy on the Romantics and the Victorians and short on the Moderns, do to our sensibility.

Siri Gunasinghe wrote some good poetry in the past. He is included in *An Anthology of Modern Writing from Sri Lanka* edited by Ranjini Obeyesekere and Chitra Fernando. [26] Poems like "Renunciation," "Dirty Dishwater," and "The Water Buffalo," display a varied range and convey a feel for life in Sri Lanka. It is a pity, therefore, that Gunasinghe has stopped writing poetry. He has reportedly said that as a professor at the University of Victoria, he has become too comfortable. Unfortunately, immigration does choke creativity in many artists. We know about so many very talented writers, singers, musicians, painters and dancers who have given up, finding the transition between cultures and places too traumatic. Siri Gunasinghe's talent, then, has to be written off as a promise of the past.

Suwanda Sugunasiri, better known for his short fiction in Sinhala, has taken to writing poetry of late. His poems, published in the *Toronto South Asian Review,* show a remarkale control of the medium. He writes about his experience as a visible minority, about his fears and hopes for his children, and about events taking place in Sri Lanka. One hopes to read more poetry from him.

These poets from Sri Lanka are making a valuable contribution to the mosaic of Canadian culture. Their poetry, for all the strengths and weaknesses, is interesting and different. Their work, when put beside that of their "Canadian" contemporaries, raises questions that deserve to be seriously considered. These questions about ideology, about domination, about race and about class have been ignored for too long by the mainstream critics and academics.

# NOTES

[1] Sam Solecki, "Michael Ondaatje," *Descant* , 14 (1983), 78.

[2] Ibid., p. 79.

[3] Ibid., p. 78.

[4] Michael Ondaatje, *the man with seven toes* (Toronto: Coach House Press, 1969).

[5] Ondaatje, *Coming Through Slaughter* (Toronto: Anansi, 1976).

[6] Ann Wilson " 'Coming Through Slaughter': Storyville Twice Told," *Descant*, 14 (1983), 103.

[7] Ibid., p. 103.

[8] Quoted in Donald M. Marquis, *In Search of Buddy Bolden: First Man of Jazz* (Baton Rouge and London: Louisiana State U P, 1978), pp. 109-110.

[9] Ondaatje, *The Collected Works of Billy the Kid: Left Handed Poems* (Toronto: Anansi, 1970).

[10] Ondaatje, *Running in the Family* (Toronto: McClleland and Stewart, 1982).

[11] Qadri Ismail, untitled review, *Kaduwa* (Journal of the University of Ceylon), 1 (1983,) 44-45.

[12] Yasmine Gooneratne, "Cultural Interaction in Modern Sri Lankan Poetry Written in English," in *Only Connect: Literary Perspectives East and West,* ed. G. Amirtanayagam and S.C. Harrex (Australia: Flinders U, 1981), p. 186.

[13] Ibid., p. 189.

[14] Rienzi Crusz, "Faces of the Sun-Man," *Eephant and Ice* (Erin, Ont.: Porcupine's Quill, 1980), pp. 35-36.

[15] Crusz, *Singing Against the Wind* (Porcupine's Quill, 1984).

[16] Ibid.

[17] Crusz, *Elephant and Ice,* p. 94

[18] Ibid., p. 90.

[19] Asoka Weerasinghe, *Home Again Lanka* (Ottawa: Commoner's, 1981), p. 26.

[20] Weerasinghe, *Poems for Jeannie* (Cornwall, Ont.: Vesta Publications, 1976), pp. 58-59.

[21] Krisantha Sri Bhaggiyadatta, *Domestic Bliss* (Toronto: Domestic Bliss, 1981).

[22] Bhaggiyadatta, unpublished mss.

[23] Charles Altieri, *Enlarging the Temple: New Directions in American Poetry During the 1960s* (Lewisburg: Bucknell UP, 1979).

[24] Bhaggiyadatta, unpublished mss.

[25] Tyrrell Mendis, *Broken Petals* (London: The Mitre Press, 1963).

[26] Ranjini Obeyesekere and Chitra Fernando, ed., *An Anthology of Modern Writing from Sri Lanka,* (Tucson, Ariz.: The U of Arizona P, 1981).

# *Digging Up the Mountains:* Bissoondath's Doomed World

*Digging Up the Mountains,* [1] a collection of fourteen short stories by Trinidad-born Neil Bissoondath, adds another name to the sizeable list of Caribbean writers who have chosen Canada as their home.

Though Bissoondath came to Canada in 1973 at the age of 18, all but two stories deal with the Caribbeans. However, only two stories name Trinidad as a specific locale. In the rest of the stories the locale either remains nameless, leaving the reader to guess for herself through the help of suggestive clues such as names, topography or weather; or it is called "the island" or "the Caribbeans." I take this deliberate blurring of specific details as a suggestion on the writer's part that the situations and events described in these stories can pertain to all the Caribbean countries. Indeed, the blurb on the front jacket of the book would have us apply these stories to "the shifting politics of the Third World" in general.

The characters in these stories have one common link: they are in various stages of transit. The island, Mr. Ramgoolam in "Insecurity" feels, is only a "temporary home" (p. 72) even though he was born there, nothing more than "a stopover." Vern's vision in "Veins Visible" can probably stand for the rootlessness of all the characters we encounter in the collection: "He saw the earth, as from space, streams of people in continuous motion, circling the sphere in search of the next stop which, they always knew, would prove temporary in the end" (p. 223).

Some of these characters have been forced to uproot themselves because of the legalized violence that, according to Bissoondath, is the way of life in the Caribbeans. The stories give the impression that the state violence is deliberately directed against the erstwhile prosperous East Indians. In the title story, Mr. Hari Beharri's friends Rangee and Faizal die mysterious deaths while he himself gets threatening phone calls in "lazy island drawl" (p. 7) and letters "typed askew on good quality papers, words often misspelt" (p. 7). Hari leads a paranoid existence, firing his gun at the mountains in the evening dusk and screaming at his would-be assailants, "Come, come and try" (p. 4).

The "black youths, wool caps pulled down tightly over their heads, impenetrable sunglasses masking their eyes" (p. 16), the Minister for State Security, "a big black man with a puffy face and clipped beard" (p. 7), and the policemen who are also black and wear the same "impenetrable glasses" arouse terror in Hari's mind in his various encounters with them. Hari finally decides to leave when his vandalized car is mockingly returned to him by the very policemen who had snatched it from him the day before.

Alistaire Ramgoolam in "Insecurity" is another prosperous East Indian who is planning to leave. He is cleverly smuggling out his money to Canada so that his son can buy a house in Toronto. Vernon in "Veins Visible" is also an East Indian who left out of fear for his life, leaving all his wealth behind him, and is now forced to paint houses in Toronto instead of hiring people to "paint *our* houses" (p. 214). These East Indians lead desperate, truncated lives in Toronto. Hari in "Veins Visible" dies in a drunken driving accident while Vernon dreams about lying on the pavement with his torso severed from the rest of his body.

The stories carry hints of deep racial divisions in the West Indies. While "Digging up the Mountains" presents the violence directly in terms of blacks as oppressors and East Indians as the oppressed, the hints in the other stories are more subtle. In "There are a Lot of Ways to Die," Joseph goes back to his native island after six years of a life of "civility" in Toronto with the idealistic motive of "starting a business, creating jobs, helping my people" (p. 90). However, the twelve workers he has hired fail to show up the day the story opens because of rain, eliciting the comment from Joseph's wife: "These people like that, you know, gal. Work is the last thing they want to do" (p. 85).

However, along with the distrust for the racially different, there is also the phenomenon of self-hatred. The black priest at Joseph's school was "the terror of all students unblessed by fair skin and athletic ability" (p. 82). Sheila, "a ordinary-fifty-dollar-a-month-maid" in "Dancing" finds a similar contradiction: "Down there Black people have Indian maid and Indian people have Black maid. . . . Black people say, Black people don't know how to work. Indian people say, Indian people always thiefing-thiefing" (p. 188).

"Dancing" is the only story in which the narrator is a black person talking about herself and her family. The stories focus mainly on East Indian characters. Perhaps that is the material Bissoondath feels most comfortable with. However, this lack of representation of black West Indians presents certain problems for a sensitive reader. As representatives of the state, the blacks are shown as terrorizing and masochistic figures. In the only story dealing with black characters in the lower walks of life, they are shown behaving most abominably. As previously mentioned, since Bissoondath has refrained from mentioning the names of particular countries, are we to presume that blacks have wrested power everywhere and the East Indians are terrorized universally? Anyone familiar with Caribbean history knows that this is not necessarily so. In fact, works such as Michael Thelwell's *Harder They Come* claim just the opposite: that the majority black population in Jamaica is oppressed by the coloured minority. I wonder if Bissoondath realized the implications of his method. The Caribbeans have a complex socio-cultural entity and lumping them together is bound to lead to distortions.

Whether it be the Caribbeans or the run-down slum houses in Toronto, or the vignettes of Europe and Japan that we see in "Continental Drift" and "The Cage," the world presented in the stories is uniformly bleak. There is no hope for redemption; individuals lead desperate, isolated lives in the absence of a viable community. "Christmas Lunch" describes a gathering of West Indians in a shabby house in Toronto by a narrator who is himself a stranger to the host and who has reluctantly joined the party hosted by his friend's friend because the prospect of the festive lunch seems preferable to the other alternative: "a blustery Christmas day in a cold room with only a book for company" (p. 163). The lunch turns out to be a pathetic travesty of the proverbial Christmas spirit of joy and harmony as the little group fails to rise above its mean day-to-day existence.

A stranger-narrator is also employed in "A Short Visit to a Failed Artist," another story about the East Indian Caribbeans in Toronto. These people, like the characters in "Christmas Lunch" and "Veins Visible," are leading fragmented, purposeless lives in a bottomless hell. However, I find it curious that the narrator, himself a West Indian, is a stranger to these characters and will probably never meet them again. One of the questions the reader might ask is whether this detached narrator is really the best vehicle for presenting these characters and whether he himself is not alienated from the joys and sorrows of this emigre community. The narrator's alienation and detachment, however, are presented without a trace of irony.

Only one short story, "Continental Drift," records a fleeting moment when human community is established. The narrator, a small-town Ontarian, suffering from "the incipient boredom" in his wanderings in Europe where prostitutes scream "Cheap fuck!" (p. 147) and empty syringes lie in the back alleys, is invited to share a meagre dinner by two young Spaniards who are looking for jobs in the French vineyards: "This one image," the narrator says, "will remain with me, will form of itself a glittering whole, will give value to an experience until now unsatisfactory" (p. 161). Once again, a reader might question why such moments of human fulfillment are not available in the Caribbeans and to the Caribbeans, especially since twelve out of the fourteen stories have to do with them. It seems a bit curious that though Europe figures only in one story it can still provide that elusive possibility of communion with one's fellow beings whereas all that goes on in the Caribbeans is "human madness" (p. 176) and "A certain stupidity" (p. 216).

If one had read these stories singly in magazines or heard them on radio broadcasts, one probably would not have noticed these disturbing meanings that arise out of juxtapositions. However, reading these fourteen stories together, one cannot but feel that certain judgements are being made without being openly articulated. The Caribbeans, we are told, have no future. The West Indians that we see in the stories have no redeeming qualities. Their lives lack even such basic civilities as love for one's family and regard for one's neighbours. Even the weather is uniformly rotten: it is rainy, foggy, steaming hot.

A corollary to this presentation is the view of Caribbean history that is voiced through one of the characters in "There are a Lot of Ways to Die": "our history does not lead anywhere. It's just a big, black hole" (p. 92). Since this view is not undercut by narrative irony or through utilization of history in other stories, one cannot but feel that it is supposed to be taken seriously. In the story, it is also reinforced by the symbolism of Pacheco house, a colonial ruin that had been built by "a crazy old man from Argentina" (p. 92) which is first declared a national monument and then allowed to go to ruin "with inexplicable murmurings of 'colonial horrors'" (p. 83). The view of the Caribbeans (or is it that of the entire Third World?) that emerges from these stories is strikingly similar to that expressed by V.S. Naipaul, Bissoondath's uncle: "a society without standards, without noble aspirations, nourished by greed and cruelty."[2]

Though it may seem unfair to generalize about the author's world view since the stories use either first person narrations or a disembodied narrative voice, the choice of subject matter, characters, symbolism, juxtapositions and narrative stance lead one to the inescapable feeling of total hopelessness. Political solutions are ridiculed. Left-wing phraseology such as "colonialism," "oppression," "American imperialism" etc. is especially under attack, at times in a most gratuitous manner and in flagrant disregard of the artistic unity of the story. While reading "The Revolutionary" one cannot help but conclude that it is not *a* Marxist that Bissoondath is attacking but all Marxists. The parody here is so exaggerated that it ceases to be funny: "'Lo-lo-look,' he stammered, imploring belief, 'you ever heard about the Popular Insurrection Service Squad? Or the Caribbean Region Association of Patriots? No? Well, them's just two of the guerilla groups. Don't think I joking, man, I dead serious now'" (p. 26). One can only surmise which political organizations are being ridiculed as PISS and CRAP. The conclusion shows "The Revolutionary" tripping on his way out and with him go down not only the Marxist gods but also the future of Trinidad:

> As he flapped his way to the door, the assistant librarian of the Future Train Movement — his head held high from pride or from the necessity of preventing his hair from crushing him — tripped over himself. Vladamir Ill Lenin, May-o, and the future of Trinidad went sprawling to the ground. (p. 29)

It is quite possible that one who does not share the author's biases will find it hard to read the stories as nothing more than aesthetic creations, to be savoured for their technical achievements exclusively. The present reader must admit to having experienced a constant sense of unease at the subtle and not so subtle ideological manipulations while reading the stories. It is not so much the violence and the corruption that I am disturbed by as by their removal from history and their presentation as the immutable condition of the Caribbeans. I cannot but disagree with the dust jacket blurb that the author has shown "a stout refusal to take sides."

Nevertheless, I do not mean to deny Bissoondath's narrative gifts. About seven of the fourteen stories are well-written and manage to sustain the reader's interest through crisp dialogue, subtle manipulation of narrative suspense, interesting characterization and evocation of detail. "Digging Up the Moun tains," "Insecurity," "Continental Drift" and "Counting the Wind" stand out especially. "Man as Plaything, Life as Mockery" and "The Cage" fail to work because of cliched situations, all-too-familiar symbolism, wooden characters and long, descriptive narrative passages. Some stories fail to provide enough motivation or explanation to allow the reader to respond to the characters' dilemmas. "Veins Visible," "A Short Visit to a Failed Artist" and "An Arrangement of Shadows" are the weakest stories in the volume.

Judging by the better stories in the collection, Bissoondath has the potential to become an important voice in Canadian fiction.

# NOTES

[1] Neil Bissondath, *Digging Up the Mountains: Selected Stories* (Toronto: Macmillan, 1985).

[2] V.S. Naipaul, *The Middle Passage* (1962; rpt. Harmondsworth: Penguin, 1969), p. 28.

# The Poetry of Rienzi Crusz: Songs of an Immigrant

Rienzi Crusz, a Sri Lankan who came to Canada in 1965, had his first collection of poems, *Flesh and Thorn*, published in 1974.[1] The second collection, *Elephant and Ice*, came out in 1980.[2] He is about to publish a third collection called *Singing Against the Wind*.[3] His poems have also been published in several national and international journals and he is the recipient of a number of awards.

It is often claimed that we are all immigrants to this land and that all Canadian literature is immigrant literature, "a mourning of homes left and things lost."[4] Such broad generalizations, however, fail to take into account cultural and racial differences among various immigrant groups and the impact of these differences on creative expression. Nor do they differentiate between the literature of the second or third generation ethnic and that of the ethnic who has arrived on these shores very recently. And such differences are not insubstantial. The problems faced by "visible" ethnics are not simply those of a traumatic severing from their past as in the case of "invisible ethnics" who do not markedly stand out from the rest of the population.[5] Furthermore, the new arrival, unlike the native-born ethnic, is bound to be preoccupied with his own sense of identity rather than with exploring his "genealogy" or with "ancestorseek[ing]."[6]

Rienzi Crusz's poetry is a good indication of how important these differences are. His poetry is an assertion of his difference. Like Yeats, he has created his own mythology and rhetoric because the available conventions of Anglo-Canadian poetry do not serve his needs. It is this act of self-creation that makes his poetry so interesting. Like so many other Third World Calibans who must perforce speak Prospero's tongue, Crusz wrestles with its inadequacies in order to communicate with the world from the vantage point of his otherness.

Crusz wears his otherness on his shoulder. There are frequent references to his skin colour in his poetry:

> Dark I am,
> and darkly do I sing
> with mucus
> in my throat
> (*EAI,* p. 90)

In another poem he speaks of his "black tongue" (*SAW*), an acute image for his separateness. Elsewhere he calls himself a "crow" (*EAI*, p.53), a black bird whose frequent recurrence in Crusz reminds one of several West Indian poets.

This self-definition makes us feel that we are in a new territory here. The comfortable sense of tradition which a mainstream poet enjoys in his relationship with the readers from a similar cultural background, and which performs half of our labour for us — familiar allusions, a shared past, binding conventions — is unavailable to Crusz for it, being alien, will only falsify his meaning. We see Crusz doing a tight-rope walk: speaking honestly in his unfamiliar "black tongue" but trying to be careful at the same time so as not to lapse into complete obscurity or nostalgia, traps immigrant writers can so easily fall into.

Certainly, there are times when the tight rope gets the better of Crusz. He does become clumsily nostalgic at times. He also indulges in exoticism. His poetry is full of evocations of the beauty of Sri Lanka such as these:

> blue Ceylon,
> where palms bend
> their coconut breasts
> to the morning sun,
> and Nuwera-Eliya's valley
> oozes with the fragrance of tea . . .
> (*EAI*, p.36)

Many of these descriptions are no more than exuberant word-painting. However, at his best, Crusz incorporates these lovely vignettes of Sri Lanka in an overall symbolic structure. Several of his poems are built around a comparison-contrast structure in which his Sri Lankan past becomes a means of scrutinizing his life in Canada. The poem entitled "Conversations With God About My Whereabouts" is a good example of his strategy:

> True, I have almost forgotten
> the terraced symmetries
> of the rice-paddy lands.
> How the gods underfoot
> churned in time
> a golden bowl of rice.
> A loss of aesthetics, perhaps.
>
> But I am perfect now.
> They have crushed the ears of corn
> to feed my belly
> white slice by slice
> and all imperfections die
> with One-A-Day and vitamin B complex.

> (*EAI*, p. 93)

The poem juxtaposes the poet's antithetical experiences of Sri Lanka and Canada over several stanzas in which Sri Lanka seems to symbolize a life lived close to the land while Canada is associated with the bounties provided by the machine. However, as we discover in the last two stanzas, Crusz is not interested in reiterating the dualism so popular in modern Canadian poetry: organic versus mechanical, natural versus industrial. In fact, the final stanza parodies these verities:

> I AM perfect now.
>
> a brown laughing face
> in the snow,
> not the white skull
> for the flies
> in Ceylon's deadly sun.
> (*EAI*, p. 95)

When one comes across these stark images of death after the earlier, paradisical descriptions of Sri Lanka, one realizes that the poet has tricked the reader deliberately. Knowing that the reader will read the poem as a nostalgic recall of his idyllic life in the mother country — a typical theme in immigrant literature — Crusz at first leads us on and then, in the last five lines, springs his surprise forcing us to reappraise not only the meaning of the poem itself but our penchant for stock dualisms as readers.

The last five lines create several ironies. One the one hand, the poem seems to be parodying the poet's own nostalgia that generated the earlier stanzas. On the other, it could still imply a subtle criticism of the western way of life which, when it removes all "imperfections," also evades a coming to terms with the ultimate imperfection: death. Finally, the poem also seems to be suggesting that the environment created by advanced technology need not be hostile to human spirit, despite the conventional wisdom of poetry. In fact, in the poem's ecology, it is paradisical nature which turns killer.

Poems like "Conversations with God About My Whereabouts" are a good indication of the strategies an immigrant poet must adopt to successfully integrate the two modes of his existence. Perhaps no native-born Canadian poet has to constantly struggle with these dualities. Crusz's choice of titles itself indicates the magnitude of his struggle. The first two titles, namely *Flesh and Thorn* and *Elephant and Ice*, bring together two antithetical elements while the latest one, *Singing Against the Wind*, emphasizes the isolation the poet feels in an environment that remains alien to his sensibility.

This sense of being an outsider, of not belonging to the charmed inner circle results in a poetic stance that speaks in understatements and mild ironic thrusts rather than the impassioned hectoring which a Layton or an Atwood might feel no qualms about because of their positions of authority. I find it interesting here that Crusz rarely uses the pronoun "we" in its inclusive sense, a rhetorical device which allows the user to speak for the entire society. This difference, it would seem, is a characteristic response of the writers coming from minority or marginalized groups. Myrna Kostash, a Ukrainian-Canadian writer speaking in a panel on "Hyphenated Canadians: The Question of Consciousness" at a conference on "Ethnicity and the Writer in Canada" defines it well:

> A negative feature of my book that some people picked up was the defensiveness of tone and a tendency to overstate my case. I can see how that could be interpreted as an ethnic characteristic, a sort of ghetto reaction, but it could also just as easily apply to the fact that I'm a Canadian vis a vis the American empire. . . . Similar ly, is the defensiveness I show in writing about Two Hills a female character istic. . . ? I am a female voice in a wilderness of masculine suprem acy, so in the end, I don't know. But this generalized condition of somehow being an outsider, of being down and outer, does come through. [7]

This difference between the tonalities of the outsider and the insider in any particular society is an intriguing one and literary critics need to become more aware of its consequences for the overall pattern of a work. The outsider, as Myrna Kostash points out, can never be sure of the right tone to adopt. If she is defensive and tending towards overstatement, Crusz's reaction is just the opposite. Unlike several other South Asian-Canadian poets who might at times appear to be almost hysterical, Crusz constantly hedges behind understatements, even when a scream might seem to be a more natural response, and instead of making any direct observations on the host society, he structures his poems as journies of the self: the self as it undergoes transformations in the new environment becomes a means of judging unobtrusively. Another related aspect of his approach is that the poems, instead of communicating with the reader on some topic of mutual interest, make statements about how difficult communication is, given the differences between the readers and the poet:

> It would have been somewhat different
> in green Sri Lanka, where I touched
> the sun's fire daily
> with my warm finger tips.

I wouldn't have hesitated
to call you a bastard
and for emphasis, might have even
thrown in the four-letter word.
(*SAW*, " in the idiom of the sun")

The efforts at softening a rather unpalatable message are very characteristic of Crusz. Even on the question of racism, a very important theme for several South Asian writers in Canada and one which provokes extreme poetic anger from many of them, Crusz's response is couched in understatements. This is how the poet describes his encounter with racists on a Toronto street:

Who, brown and strolling
down a Toronto street
came up against these black vinyl jackets
with mouths hurling their PAKI PAKI words like knives;
Froze, then quickly thawed to his notebook:
"Color of offenders' eyes: hazel, blue, blue.
Hair: All long, like Jesus, down the nape.
Estimated educational background: T.V.' s 'Police Story,'
Starring Angie Dickinson.
Home Address: Paradise Blvd. , Toronto
Possible motives: kicks
So much poetry in the trajectory of crow sounds."
(*SAW*, "The Sun Man's Poetic Five Ways")

This composure in the face of extreme provocation is characteristic of Crusz. "[W]ords like knives" and "Froze" are the only two indications in the stanza of the pain and fear caused by racial attitudes. The poetic act of containment also suggests the price which the brown-skinned immigrant pays for maintaining a dignified front. The feelings of hate and anger must somehow be transmuted into laughter if one wants to function in the day-to-day world:

When hate wears
a white mud mask,
and dances in rituals
of living death,
he holds out a golden hand
marinated in the sun,
a Jesus heart plucked
From some ancient Calvary.
(*EAI*, p. 35)

I find it interesting here that Crusz, instead of directly accusing the victim-izer, personifies hate, thereby sublimating his anger, a posture which some South Asian poets reject in favour of spilling out their outrage. Both responses, of course, are resorted to by the visible minorities.

Congruent with his response to racism is Crusz's response to colonialism, another important theme in the work of South Asian poets in Canada. Some of them lash out at what they consider to be the complacency and the insularity of Canadian society in this regard. They write poems on historical events as well as the present political turmoil in the Third World. Crusz, characteristically, understates the theme. For example, the short poem entitled "Roots," which is ostensibly about the poet's mixed parentage, becomes a vehicle for an oblique comment on Sri Lanka's colonial history:

> A Portuguese captain holds
> the soft brown hand of my Sinhala mother,
> It's the year 1515 A.D.,
> When two civilizations kissed and merged,
> and I, burgher of that hot embrace,
> write a poem of history
> as if it were only the romance
> of a lonely soldier on a crowded beach
> in Southern Ceylon.
>
> (*SAW*, "Roots")

Here again we see Crusz's penchant for overturning the reader's stock expectations and making him sit up in surprise. The subordinate conjunctions opening the seventh line rewrite the entire poem into the ironic mode, displacing its romantic surface. The poet appears to chide himself for having romanticised history by converting it into a love story. Nevertheless, that aspect, though qualified, is not completely denied as it retains validity in the poet's personal life. The poem, thus, speaks of the paradoxical relationship of the Burghers to Sri Lanka. Of a mixed parentage, the Burghers have felt torn in both directions: unable to denounce the colonizers as vociferously as their fellow countrymen since they also happened to be ancestors, yet conscious of their exploitative role. Crusz's poem captures this dilemma very poignantly.

This process of rewriting, undercutting, and qualifying by means of one or two strategic words is so subtle that an unwary reader, beguiled by the otherwise transparent surface, could miss the underlying ironies quite easily. For example, this reference to ivory in a poem called "The Maker" is highly elliptical:

> And I am made
> ready

95

for the Sahara,
with a black ugly beak
that knows there's water
trembling in the cactus,

. . .
ready
for the white hunter
heavy with ivory dream,
as he strokes his elephant-gun
and waits for the color of dawn.

(*EAI*, pp. 53-4)

For this reader, "the white hunter/ heavy with ivory dream" strongly recalls Conrad's *Heart of Darkness*. The allusion, used with tremendous precision, interweaves the personal and the historical. While this allusion has its source in a well known writer, many of Crusz's allusions are picked from non-western literary and cultural traditions and may appear obscure to an unprepared reader. However, this obscurity in the South Asian poet stems from his decision to remain honest to his experience. Thus, poems like "Sermon in the Forest" (*EAI*, pp. 68-70), "Baby-Photo Inc vs Michael Egerton Crusz," and "dark antonyms in paradise" (SAW), might puzzle the non-South Asian readers, both in terms of their belief systems and language. The following lines from "dark antonyms in paradise" serve as a good example:

. . . what media
and the London Economist declared
was the new redemption, the prosperity
Hongkong and Singapore style.
How JR, like the great Dutugemunu
builds another brazen palace
by the marshes of Kotte,
and now rests in his silken sarong
and ripened dreams.

(*SAW*)

The poem demands a certain level of acquaintance with Sri Lanka's past and present. It demands that the reader do some home work of his own. For example, when I found out who "Dutugemunu" was from a Sri Lankan friend of mine, the poem's ironies multiplied. The comparison of the Sri Lankan President, Jayawardene, with an illustrious and ostentatious Sinhala king who defeated the Tamil king Elara and built a gold-coloured palace is wonderfully subtle as it obliquely refers to the current racial strife in Sri Lanka as well as to the rather extravagant expenditures on the new parliament buildings by Jayawardene's government.

A related aspect of Crusz's poetry, and one that he shares with other South-Asian Canadian poets, is the use of references to artists and art forms of the Third World. This, again, is a poetic act that declares Crusz's sense of solidarity with the people of the Third World. "At Chalkie's Calypso Tent" pays tribute to the Calypso artists of Port-of-Spain and attempts to communicate their rhythms and satiric thrusts:

> And bald Smiley,
> champion of the poor,
> your Economy song
> came through so clear,
> a solution for the arse
> which could do well with water
> instead of British toilet paper.
>
> (*EAI*, p. 73)

Thus, the main referents in Crusz's poetry are from his Third World background. He is trying to communicate, through the use of these unfamiliar images, allusions, rhythms and structures, what it is to be an immigrant and a non-white in a society that is so dissimilar from that of one's origin. His "Immigrant's Song" (*EAI*, p. 49) is not only an attempt to come to terms with his own past, it is also a heroic statement of poetic independence. While to his South Asian readers Crusz brings consolations of a fellow immigrant who understands and gives voice to their reality and their loss, to other Canadians he brings a beneficial encounter with otherness, an insight into other ways of perceiving the world.

It is high time the mainstream, as it is called, took note of these voices like that of Crusz from the outer periphery of Canadian life. Things as they stand now are pretty hegemonic. For example, Margaret Atwood's *The New Oxford Book of Canadian Verse in English* (1982) includes only two minority figures. However, in neither Michael Ondaatje nor Pier Giorgio Di Cicco ethnicity becomes a major theme. Canadian Literature curricula at the universitites are equally blank when it comes to the contributions of immigrant writers in general and non-white writers in particular. Such neglect is highly unfortunate for it encourages a rather narrow, ethnocentric view of literature — and, ultimately, of society itself— insensitive to unfamiliar voices and incestuously self-enclosed. The loss is especially deplorable in the case of immigrant writers from the Third World, writers who have been exposed to non-western traditions of writing. Their poetry, if heard, could spark new areas of critical inquiry:

97

the relationship of the poet to his tradition, the nature of differences between traditions, the culture-bound nature of poetic language and symbolism, and the nature of a poet's relationship with his audience. These, of course, are matters of technique. The voices of the coloured immigrant poets are important also because they report on Canadian society from a vantage point that is not available to a well-adjusted, native-born, "invisible" Canadian. They make their poetry out of what I would like to call the areas of silence in Canadian writing.

# NOTES

[1] Rienzi Crusz, *Flesh and Thorn* (Stratford, Ontario: The Pasdeloup Press, 1974).

[2] Crusz, *Elephant and Ice* (Erin, Ontario: The Porcupine's Quill , 1980). Hereafter cited in the article as *EAI*.

[3] Crusz, *Singing Against the Wind*. To be published by The Porcupine's Quill. Quotations from the collection cited herein are from unpaginated mss. kindly supplied to this writer by Mr. Crusz. References in the text are identified by the title of the poem preceded by *SAW*.

[4] Margaret Atwood, "Introduction," *The New Oxford Book of Canadian Verse in English*, ed. Margaret Atwood (Toronto: Oxford University Press, 1982), p. xxxi.

[5] Editorial, "On Visibility," *Canadian Literature*, 95 (Winter 1982), 2-3, 4,5.

[6] Robert Kroetsch, Tamara J. Palmer and Beverly J. Rasporich, "Editorial: Ethnicity and Canadian Literature," *Canadian Ethnic Studies*, 14: 1 (1982), iii.

[7] Myrna Kostash quoted in Jars Balan, ed. *Identifications: Ethnicity and the Writer in Canada,* (Edmonton: The Canadian Institute of Ukrainian Studies, The University of Alberta, 1982), p. 151.

# The Third World in the Dominant Western Cinema:
## Responses of a Third World Viewer

Recent feminist criticism of dominant cinema has shown how it constructs images of women to suit the psychological needs of the male spectator and the male filmmaker. The woman is contained, co-opted, and often dismembered so that the male needs of dominance and status quo can be satisfied. The feminists insist that what we see on the screen are male fantasies of what a woman ought to be. The cinema cleverly displaces the conflicts of male-female relations in the real world and contains the intransigent woman through its narrative and cinematic techniques. Sometimes it succeeds so well that the female spectator gives her allegiance to it.[1]

As a female viewer, I have no difficulty in sympathising with the analysis of the western feminists. However, as a Third World viewer, occupying a marginal space in places like the media and the universities, I have other concerns which I consider to be more wide-ranging. My concerns are with the misrepresentation, manipulation and fantasization of the people of the Third World. It is not only my sex that the western films demean, but my culture, history and racial being as well — if the individualisitic west can understand such a thing as the collective being.

Of late there has been a spate of films, television serials, songs and novels about the Third World. They join in with the images of the starving, the sick and the dying whom the likes of Mother Teresa administer. One needs also to add to these images the voices of people like Ronald Reagan and George Schultz who tell the naughty, socialist-minded Third World leaders that they will never be able to raise their countries above the dung-heap if they don't adopt the capitalistic ways.

What is, of course, hidden behind these images and pronouncements is the bitter history of colonialism. However, what is not admitted does not go away but keeps hovering like Banquo's ghost at the banquet. No matter how many fathoms deep the white man tries to bury his burden, it continues to surface unrepressed. Or else, why make films like "A Passage to India," "Gods Must Be Crazy," "Out of Africa" and "Crocodile Dundee"?

Of course, there is nothing wrong with facing one's past and coming to terms with it. If one does it honestly, one can lay to rest the nagging anguish caused by the sins of omission and commission, and get on with the business of living. To a certain extent, that does happen in "Gandhi." It is an honest movie which takes an unflinching look at the past. Whatever its shortcomings, it is a film that continues to attract me and retains its appeal through multiple viewings. It is because I feel that the filmmaker respected the country and the people he was portraying and allowed them to speak in their own voice.

This is not what one can say about "A Passage to India," "Out of Africa" and "Gods Must be Crazy." What I see happening in these films is the white man's attempt to exorcize the past and to make it appear as though the bad part — the sin and guilt part — never happened. What I see happening in these films is cultural recolonization, an attempt to go back to the place of one's past crime and recreate the past in a way that the crime is displaced, muffled, washed out.

That impulse, of course, is there in much of white man's literature. The question is, how to do what has to be done and stop the naggings of the guilt-ridden conscience? In James Fennimore Cooper's novel, *Deerslayer,* Natty Bumpo, the good white man, kills an Indian in self-defence, and the dying Indian utters a benediction absolving Bumpo of the guilt. As Peter Abrahams has David Brown, the black pastor, say in *The View from Coyaba:* "It is not enough to take what is mine. You want me to tell you it is right for you to do it."[2]

That is what happens in all the three films I want to look at. The white man in them wants the Third World native to tell him that it was all right for him to have taken away the victim's birthright, that it was indeed good for the native that the white man came to his country and "civilized" him. And if the Third World native refuses to do it in the real world — just look at the voting records of the Third World countries in the U.N. — the white man will construct images of him in the imaginary world of art and make him perform the desired genuflections.

These films use many subtle and not so subtle techniques of cinematic discourse to present an aesthetic experience that is demeaning and infuriating for the Third World viewer. These devices include distortions of history and contemporary reality, subtle omissions, imposition of the perennial western form of romance, caricature of the native people's viewpoints and characters, exoticization of their land, and presentation of the western characters as larger than life and benevolent educators. Most westerners do not see the racist and imperialist designs of these aesthetic experiences. As well, they dismiss the Third World viewer's responses as "ideological," and "too political," art supposedly being free from ideology and politics.

"A Passage to India," for example, was lauded whole-heartedly in the media as another of David Lean's classics and awarded its share of Oscars. Most of my white friends commented on how beautiful the photography was, how lovely the Indian landscapes. Of course, there were a few deviations from the Forster novel, but then the filmmaker is allowed to take a few liberties, they said. The more astute among them reacted negatively to the clown-like portrayal of Professor Godbole and the happy ending where Aziz bids farewell to his white friends in the most submissive manner. But the portrayal of the Third World is not a matter of identity crisis for them as it is to us, products of the soil, visible carriers of its stamp upon our skins, our features, our minds. They went back to teaching the canonical works of English and American literature, popular literature being a pariah at our universities, along with questions of racism and imperialism.

One cannot go back to these higher pursuits, however, if one has a child who must go to see films like "Gods Must Be Crazy" and "Crocodile Dundee" because all his other classmates have seen them. One must sit through the films, feeling like a spoilsport and a weirdo, because everyone else seems to be laughing their heads off. And finally, one must go through an impassioned session of discussions with a nine year old child, to make him aware of the indignities perpetrated on his kind of people in the name of harmless fun. One feels a sense of profound alienation at such times. One writes to counter that alienation and to put on record that the discourse of cultural imperialism is not the only discourse.

What, then, bothers one most? Perhaps it is the all-pervasive narrative structure of a white man loving a white woman in an exotic tropical landscape filled with equally exotic natives. The centre of all the three films is this romance, embellished with strains of classical western music. What is at a premium is the sexuality of the white characters, hauntingly explored. The cinematic experience is entirely devoted to the tensions of the heterosexual romance. All else is secondary.

Thus, in "A Passage to India," Lean shifts the focus away from Dr. Aziz, who is the true hero of the Forster novel and turns it on Adela, with whom he opens the film. Lean manufactures a rather tacky section in which Adela sees erotic sculptures in the wilderness, supposedly "to let you see she is beginning to awaken sexually . . . because India can do this you know."[3] The section subtly changes and depoliticizes the toughest aspects of Forster's novel. In the film, Adela is overpowered by this erotic awakening to such an extent that she dares to talk to Aziz about "love" and asks him whether he "loved" his wife. His reply to this is, "We were young, and we were a man and a woman." In the book, however, the conversation is not so civilized. Instead of talking about "love," Adela asks Dr. Aziz: "Have you one wife or more than one?"[4] It is this insensitive question that leads to disaster and not Adela's sexual awakening. Stung, muttering, "Damn the English even at their best," Aziz plunges into one of the caves "to recover his balance."[5]

The film, however, sweetens the imperialistic relations of the British and the Indians to mere social misunderstanding. The "bridge party" is seen as a personal failure of the Turtons who just happen to be bad-mannered. Mrs. Moore's acid comments about" an exercise in power and the subtle pleasures of personal superiority" somehow make it all right to have an empire if only one exercized good manners. The book is much tougher on Mrs. Moore.

The "love" talk helps Lean to rewrite the  court scene in an idiom as tacky as the fake erotic sculptures. Lean tells us that Ronny has willingly stepped down as magistrate in Das's favour because of the stringent requirements of British justice and sense of fair play and not because, as the novel has it, the Indian defence lawyers have demanded it. Finally, there is a long, awkward statement from Adela about her "intimate" conversation with Aziz  about "love" and how she came to realize that she and Ronny did not love each other. It is Adela's sexuality, her western cultural values about love as essential for marriage that gain the centre of the stage, obliterating her insensitive assault on Aziz's sensibility.

Focussing the film on Adela's sexual misadventure allows Lean to decentre Dr. Aziz. How does it matter to him if Aziz is the first character to whom we are introduced in the novel, or that the book also closes with him, aloof and intransigent? The Aziz we meet in the film is a wimp and not one who, " like all Indians," is "skilful in the slighter impertinences."[6] Thus, in the book, when Mrs. Turton and Mrs. Lesley appropriate Aziz's tonga without even noticing him, let alone asking him, he subtly, ironically underscores their rudeness by commenting: "You are most welcome, ladies."[7] The film allows no such "impertinences." This attitude is what, probably, made Victor Bannerjee, the Indian movie actor playing Aziz, comment bitterly on the Hollywoodian imperatives of the film.

One of the major final let downs of the film comes when we see Fielding and Stella projected against the Himalayas with loud background music and a submissive Aziz bidding them goodbye. The novel admitted that power relationships cannot be transformed into friendships. The film papers over this profound statement in a most awkward and disturbing manner. What else can one expect from a producer/director who believes in the white man's burden? Lean comments in an interview that he deliberately "toned down" the novel's hatred towards the British Raj." It's all very well to criticise the English but just take a look at New Delhi, look at the railway system, look at the postal system — which works. We've left them all sorts of bad things, I suppose, but they also got some very good things."[8]

Not only does Aziz embrace Fielding, unlike the bitter and vitriolic Aziz of the novel, we hear his voice reading a conciliatory letter to Adela asking her to "forgive him." It is a very subtle manipulation of the semi-humorous, semi-ironic letter he writes in the novel. Of course, he never asks her to "forgive him." Nor does he say: "It has taken me all this time for me to appreciate your courage." The poor native, it took him two years to learn his manners. The film ends with Adela back in England, standing against a window, as the rain falls soothingly outside. As Michael Sragow so approvingly puts it: "It's as if, with its wild panoramic beauty and apocalyptic catastrophes, her time in India was a primal dream — a dream she now carries with her, every waking hour."[9]

What a nice closure! The native is put where he belongs — in the "primal dream" that comes to disturb one's tranquillity once in a while. One can continue with the business of daily living once one has contained the native in this dream space. In fact, it is a double containment. The native is relegated to the subordinate role in the dream structure of the film and then further relegated to the dim memory of the white character gone back to the Metropolis.

This is what a Third World viewer sees in films like "Gods Must Be Crazy," "Out of Africa" and "Crocodile Dundee." The native in all these films is the white man's fantasy of the noble savage, naked and painted, content in his habitat. Mick Dundee of "Crocodile Dundee" is the fantasy white man who lives in harmony with nature and is at home with the natives. He even paints his face and participates in the ritual midnight dance in the recesses of the wilderness. As to the aborigines' land claims, he says: "The aborigines don't own the land; the land owns them."

The natives in "Gods Must Be Crazy" are equally content. Only, the reality of apartheid is a lot uglier. As anthropologists Richard B. Lee and Toby Volkman point out, "The Bushman as Noble Savage is a peculiar piece of white South African racial mythology."[10] They demonstrate the contrasts between the fantasy !Kung San of the film and the way they really are in the 1980s. "There is . . . little to laugh about in Bushmanland: 1000 demoralized, formerly independent foragers crowd into a squalid, tubercular homeland, getting by on handouts of cornmeal and sugar, drinking Johnnie Walker or home brew, fighting with one another and joining the South African army."[11]

Such dissenting opinions have not been on the forefront of media coverage. The film has been a run away success in Toronto. And it is not just children who like it. Some colleagues of mine in the English department of an Ontario university could not see an ounce of racism in it. The film was for them an example of pure comedy and a living symbol of their belief that art and politics have nothing to do with each other. They could not see why the noble savage living an innocent, non-materialistic, non-urban life was offensive to me. For them the film was an unabashed criticism of the complex, machine-dependent urban life.

The stated and unstated meanings I see as a Third World viewer are much closer to the ones pointed out by Lee and Volkman than to ones seen by my fellow teachers of literature. It is galling to me to be told that !Kung San are content in their habitat when they don't even have one.

But the fantasy of the white man does not stop at the noble savage bit. His guilt, very much like Cooper's, makes him portray the native as voluntarily rejecting such bounties of civilization as the Coca-Cola bottle. Now what could be neater than that? The white man can enjoy his consumerism and standard of life without worrying about the native's poverty because not only does he like his poverty, but also because he rejects material goods since they destroy his harmonious life style. What could be a better salve for the white man's conscience?

Equally interesting for a Third World viewer are the clownish portrayal of Marxist revolutionaries who are ineffective, stupid as well as barbaric. They destroy the otherwise paradisical countryside in their frantic and meaningless flight from the forces of law and order. A Third World viewer wonders whether these are wishful portrayals of Mozambicans, Angolans, Namibians and ANC guerrillas. And how convenient to use the native to destroy his own country-men. The insurgents are captured with the help of the Bushman hero's devices. Meanwhile the two whites in the film pursue such high-minded subjects as scientific experiments on elephant dung, dissemination of education to the benighted natives and, finally, romance.

The film is an out and out insult to the aspirations of the Third World people as a whole and particularly to the African people struggling for justice. It is disconcerting for a non-white Canadian to find that this longest running first-run movie in cities like New York and Toronto, has won acclaim from the pundits.

Although a non-white living in North America must face several types of blatant and not so blatant racism, it is the cultural racism of the subtle kind that hurts the most. "Gods Must Be Crazy," "A Passage to India" and "Out of Africa" are supposedly "better" movies. They do not propagate racism openly. In fact they are so seductive as depictions of lost paradises that they tend to disarm an unwary viewer. After all, what can be more apolitical than a man and a woman falling in or out of love? To the western audience saturated with this theme, the films may seem totally innocuous, no more than travel promotion for these countries. In fact, many people, including my gas-meter reader, have commented to me about the lush natural beauty of India and Kenya as depicted in "A Passage to India" and "Out of Africa." The films obviously did nothing more for these people than to provoke a vague desire to visit these countries.

However, that is not how Third World viewers watched them. There were angry responses in India and Kenya. India banned "Gods Must Be Crazy" on grounds of racism. According to *The Toronto Star* of March 26, 1986, Kenyans considered "Out of Africa" to be a "a demeaning racist movie." It is interesting to contrast these reactions to those of North American reviewers who, while acknowledging that "Out of Africa" paid no attention to the greediest land grab, spoliation and disinheritance, went on to speak about its "epic" reach, its "sensuous" and "sensual" qualities. Their attention was focussed on the romantic couple in the lap of nature. These two elements, sexuality and the grand sweep of the landscape, were what stuck to their imagination.

But what does stick in the mind of a non-white viewer? Sam Kahiga, the Kenyan reviewer quoted in *The Toronto Star*, was deeply offended by the "positive image" of Lord Delamare, a man who once killed two Africans by running them down when they failed to jump away from his car in time. Kahiga says, "Such are the characters *Out of Africa* honoured."

It is instructive for non-whites and concerned whites to read what N'Gugi had to say about Isak Dinesen's *Out of Africa* in his book *Detained*. As he shows, Dinesen used an extensive animal imagery to portray Africans. His most acute criticism of Dinesen pertains to her use of Africa as a background for her erotic fantasies.[12]

There is no space in these films for the experience of victimization perpetrated by colonialism. No effort is made to sort out the mess of history. The Third World viewer feels nothing but a profound alienation and degradation upon seeing such films. The non-white viewer can only react with anger when, after seeing the marginalization and caricature of African people throughout "Out of Africa," he or she hears Karen Blixen's voice-over in Meryl Streep's fake Danish accent: "If I know a song of Africa, of the giraffe, and the African new moon lying on her back, of the ploughs in the fields and the sweaty faces of the coffee pickers, does Africa know a song of me? Would the air over the plain quiver with a colour that I had had on, or the children invent a game in which my name was, or the full moon throw a shadow over the gravel of the drive that was like me, or would the eagles of Ngong look out for me?"[13] This emotional self-indulgence is a masterful example of possessive individualism. Of course, Africans remember Dinesen, but not in the images of high romanticism as she would have wanted. N'Gugi's ruthless criticism of her writings is a perfect antidote for the sick sentimentality of the film.

At the PEN Conference in New York last year, Salman Rushdie was accused by angry American writers of being "prescriptive" when he suggested that American novelists should also write about their country's imperialistic relationship with the developing countries.[14] Indeed, that is a question many of us have on our minds. How is it that the west keeps churning out works about attenuated sensibilities while disregarding the havoc caused by relations of imperialism in the less privileged parts of the world? And then, to add insult to injury, not only does it deny its complicity, it transforms our denuded, depredated earth into a colourful backdrop against which the drama of attenuated sensibilities can be played and re-played.

As long as such relationships prevail, a Third World viewer like myself can only feel what Aziz feels at the end of Forster's novel: "Aziz in an awful rage danced this way and that, not knowing what to do, and cried: 'Down with the English anyhow. That's certain. Clear out, you fellows, double quick, I say. We may hate one another, but we hate you most. If I don't make you go, Ahmed will, Karim will, if it's fifty or five hundred years, we shall get rid of you, yes, we shall drive every blasted Englishman into the sea, and then, . . . and then,' he concluded, half kissing him [Fielding], 'you and I shall be friends.' As the Mau sky and the earth say, in their hundred voices, 'No, not yet,' . . . 'No, not there'."[15]

However honey-sweet  the discourse of these films, it does not make us friends. Their fictional space is as unsuitable for friendship and understanding as Mau. They only lead to heartache and anguish and a long chain of misunderstandings.

# NOTES

1  These concepts are presented in Annette Kuhn's *Women's Pictures: Feminism and Cinema* ( London: Routledge and Kegan Paul,1982).

2 Peter Abrahams, *The View from Coyaba* (London: Faber and Faber, 1982), p. 117.

3 David Lean interviewed by Harlan Kennedy, "I'm a Picture Chap," *Film Comment,* 21: 1, January/February, 1985, p. 30.

4 E.M. Forster, *A Passage to India,* ed. Oliver Stallybrass. (1924; Harmondsworth: Penguin, 1986), p. 164.

5 *Ibid.,* p. 164.

6 *Ibid.,* p. 296.

7 *Ibid.,* p. 39

8 "I'm a Picture Chap," p. 32.

9 Michael Sragow, "David Lean's Right of 'Passage'," *Film Comment,* 1985, 21: 1, January/February, p. 27

10 Toby Volkman, Letter to *The New York Times,* reprinted in *Southern Africa Report,* June, 1985, p. 20.

11 Volkman, p. 20.

12 Ngugi Wa Thiong'o, *Detained: A Writer's Prison Diary* (London: Heinemann, 1981), see pp. 34-38.

13 Quoted verbatim in the film from Isak Dinesen (1937,1954; Harmondsworth: Penguin, 1985), p. 64

14 Reported by A. Sikri, *India Abroad ,* June 24, 1986.

15 *A Passage to India,* pp. 314-5.

# ARUN MUKHERJEE

Arun Mukherjee came to Canada from India in 1971 as a Commonwealth Scholar. She did her graduate work in English at the Univesity of Toronto, obtaining her Ph. D in 1981. She is the author of *The Gospel of Weath in the American Novel* (1987) as well as several critical articles and stories. She is an Assistant Professor in the Division of Humanities, York University, North York.

Arun lives in Toronto with her husband, Alok and their ten year old son, Gautam.

# Publishing History of Articles in
## *Towards an Aesthetic of Opposition*

Seven of the essays contained in this collection have been previously published elsewhere, some under somewhat different titles. The author is pleased to acknowledge their publishing history.

"The Vocabulary of the 'Universal': Cultural Imperialism and Western Literary Criticism," *World Literature Written in English*, 26: 2 (1986).

"Ideology in the Classroom: A Case Study in the Teaching of English Literature in Canadian Universities," *Dalhousie Review*, 66: 1/2 (1986).

"Two Responses to Otherness: The Poetry of Michael Ondaatje and Cyril Dabydeen," *Journal of Commonwealth Literature*, 20: 1 (1985).

"South Asian Poetry in Canada: In Search of Place," *World Literature Written in English*, 20: 1 (1986). Also published in *A Meeting of Streams: South Asian Literature in Canada*, ed. M.G. Vassanji (Toronto: TSAR Publications, 1985).

"The Sri Lankan Poets in Canada: An Alternative View," *Toronto South Asian Review*, 3: 2 (Fall 1984).

"Songs of an Immigrant: The Poetry of Rienzi Crusz, *Currents*, 4: 1 (1986-87).

"Third World in the Dominant Western Cinema: Responses of a Third World Viewer," *Toronto South Asian Review*, 5: 3 (1987).